Knoxville, Tennessee

Written by Jacob W. Williams

Edited by Adam Burns, Meghan Dowdell, Kimberly Moore, and Jon Skindzier

Layout by Matt Hamman

Additional contributions by Omid Gohari, Christina Koshzow, Chris Mason, Joey Rahimi, and Luke Skurman

College Prowler

ISBN # 1-4274-0199-3
ISSN # 1552-1788

Printed in the U.S.A.
www.collegeprowler.com

Last Updated 5/15/06

Special Thanks To: Babs Carryer, Andy Hannah, LaunchCyte, Tim O'Brien, Bob Sehlinger, Thomas Emerson, Andrew Skurman, Barbara Skurman, Bert Mann, Dave Lehman, Daniel Fayock, Chris Babyak, The Donald H. Jones Center for Entrepreneurship, Terry Slease, Jerry McGinnis, Bill Ecenberger, Idie McGinty, Kyle Russell, Jacque Zaremba, Larry Winderbaum, Roland Allen, Jon Reider, Team Evankovich, Lauren Varacalli, Abu Noaman, Mark Exler, Daniel Steinmeyer, Jared Cohon, Gabriela Oates, David Koegler, Glen Meakem, and the University of Tennessee Bounce-Back Team.

College Prowler®
5001 Baum Blvd.
Suite 750
Pittsburgh, PA 15213

Phone: 1-800-290-2682
Fax: 1-800-772-4972
E-Mail: info@collegeprowler.com
Web Site: www.collegeprowler.com

Welcome to College Prowler®

During the writing of College Prowler's guidebooks, we felt it was critical that our content was unbiased and unaffiliated with any college or university. We think it's important that our readers get honest information and a realistic impression of the student opinions on any campus—that's why if any aspect of a particular school is terrible, we (unlike a campus brochure) intend to publish it. While we do keep an eye out for the occasional extremist—the cheerleader or the cynic—we take pride in letting the students tell it like it is. We strive to create a book that's as representative as possible of each particular campus. Our books cover both the good and the bad, and whether the survey responses point to recurring trends or a variation in opinion, these sentiments are directly and proportionally expressed through our guides.

College Prowler guidebooks are in the hands of students throughout the entire process of their creation. Because you can't make student-written guides without the students, we have students at each campus who help write, randomly survey their peers, edit, layout, and perform accuracy checks on every book that we publish. From the very beginning, student writers gather the most up-to-date stats, facts, and inside information on their colleges. They fill each section with student quotes and summarize the findings in editorial reviews. In addition, each school receives a collection of letter grades (A through F) that reflect student opinion and help to represent contentment, prominence, or satisfaction for each of our 20 specific categories. Just as in grade school, the higher the mark the more content, more prominent, or more satisfied the students are with the particular category.

Once a book is written, additional students serve as editors and check for accuracy even more extensively. Our bounce-back team—a group of randomly selected students who have no involvement with the project—are asked to read over the material in order to help ensure that the book accurately expresses every aspect of the university and its students. This same process is applied to the 200-plus schools College Prowler currently covers. Each book is the result of endless student contributions, hundreds of pages of research and writing, and countless hours of hard work. All of this has led to the creation of a student information network that stretches across the nation to every school that we cover. It's no easy accomplishment, but it's the reason that our guides are such a great resource.

When reading our books and looking at our grades, keep in mind that every college is different and that the students who make up each school are not uniform—as a result, it is important to assess schools on a case-by-case basis. Because it's impossible to summarize an entire school with a single number or description, each book provides a dialogue, not a decision, that's made up of 20 different topics and hundreds of student quotes. In the end, we hope that this guide will serve as a valuable tool in your college selection process. Enjoy!

OMID GOHARI ○ CHRISTINA KOSHZOW ○ CHRIS MASON ○ JOEY RAHIMI ○ LUKE SKURMAN ○

The College Prowler Team

UNIVERSITY OF TENNESSEE

Table of Contents

By the Numbers

General Information

University of Tennessee
800 Andy Holt Tower
Knoxville, TN 37996

Control:
Public

Academic Calendar:
Semester

Religious Affiliation:
None

Founded:
1794

Web Site:
www.utk.edu

Main Phone:
(865) 974-1000

Admissions Phone:
(865) 974-2184

Student Body

Full-Time Undergraduates:
18,065

Part-Time Undergraduates:
1,569

Total Male Undergraduates:
9,631

Total Female Undergraduates:
10,003

Admissions

Overall Acceptance Rate:
44%

Regular Acceptance Rate:
44%

Total Applicants:
10,832

Total Acceptances:
4,793

Freshman Enrollment:
4,422

Yield (% of admitted students who actually enroll):
92%

Early Decision Available?
No

Early Action Available?
Yes

Early Action Deadline:
November 1

Early Action Notification:
December 15

Regular Decision Deadline:
February 1

Regular Decision Notification:
Within 2-3 weeks

Must-Reply-By Date:
May 1

Transfer Applications Received:
2,376

Transfer Applications Accepted:
1,724

Transfer Students Enrolled:
908

Transfer Application Acceptance Rate:
73%

Common Application Accepted?
No

Supplemental Forms?
Yes

Admissions E-Mail:
admissions@utk.edu

Admissions Web Site:
http://admissions.utk.edu

SAT I or ACT Required?
Yes

SAT I Range (25th–75th Percentile):
1000–1220

SAT I Verbal Range (25th–75th Percentile):
500–610

SAT I Math Range (25th–75th Percentile):
500–610

Freshman Retention Rate:
78%

Top 10% of High School Class:
29%

Application Fee:
$25

Financial Information

In-State Tuition:
$5,376

Out-of-State Tuition:
$10,192

Room and Board:
$5,398

Books and Supplies:
$1,156

Average Need-Based Financial Aid Package (including loans, work-study, grants, and other sources):
$9,264

Students Who Applied For Financial Aid:
68%

Students Who Received Aid:
42%

Financial Aid Forms Deadline:
March 1

Financial Aid Phone:
(865) 974-3131

Financial Aid E-Mail:
finaid@utk.edu

Financial Aid Web Site:
http://web.utk.edu/~finaid

Did You Know?

Top "feeder" high schools for UT include Farragut, Bearden, Red Bank, Houston, Germantown, Ooltewah, Brentwood, Centennial, Knox West, and Soddy Daisy.

Students Speak Out On...
Academics

"Depending on your major, teachers range from highly effective to highly useless. Teachers, for most of the more popular majors, have their TAs do a considerable portion of the coursework."

"You will hear different things from different people; **it all depends on your learning style** and what type of teacher you like. There are many teachers for each subject and class, and there are many sections for each class and level. You can choose your professor rather than living with a professor you despise. UT is pretty good about weeding out the bad seeds in teaching. They don't keep professors if students don't give them good ratings."

"**Never hesitate to visit the teachers during office hours**. Some will beg you, others may not, but a visit will show an instructor that you care about the class. They will remember you and put a name with a face, which doesn't hurt around grading time. If you are lucky, they might give you test studying tips or show you extra notes."

"**The longer you spend at UT, the more of an understanding you will have** as to which teachers will be problematic. Until then, just use your basic instincts. If you can't understand them, look for another section number."

"While most of **the distribution classes seem to be large and impersonal**, the upper-level courses are the total opposite. As the classes get more in-depth in each field, both the classes and the teachers get more interesting and more individualized toward each student."

"For the most part, teachers are easy-going and really helpful. **I've never had a teacher who refused to help in any way they could**. College is very different from high school, though, so be forewarned that teachers will not remind you when something is due. You get a syllabus at the beginning of the year and it becomes your bible—do not lose it! Many teachers get really peeved if you ask for another one. Make sure you stay on top of the readings and assignments because there is no break-in time. You will have reading homework on the first day for every class—I guarantee it."

"**I've liked every single teacher I have had**. I went to a very competitive high school, so I feel like the teachers here almost baby us. They always end up curving grades, delaying due dates, and making other compromises with students. There are still a few sticklers, though, so watch out. All teachers are nice and willing to help you out after class hours anytime."

"While many teachers seem like jerks while sitting in class, **many are very friendly on an individual basis**, as long as you are not the student that constantly shows up late, sleeps in class, or never comes."

"If you ever mess up, there is one important thing to remember—most professors are like motorcycle cops. They have heard every excuse in the book, and they are usually on to any lame excuse you might make. I missed an exam in a class taught by one of the toughest instructors in the department who clearly stated in the syllabus, 'no exam make-ups. I overslept on exam day and woke up hours after it was over. I contacted the instructor, explained honestly what happened, and he allowed me to take the missed exam that day. It may not always work out this way, but **a good rule of thumb in this situation is to always be honest and show respect**."

"The teachers vary, but **you can screen them before you choose classes by getting a *Tennessee 101* guide**. They're free anywhere on campus. They tell you how the teachers were rated by their students and let you know the average grades the teachers give."

"**The teachers are as good as can be expected, considering the size of their classes**. For instance, in my chemistry lecture, I was one of about 500 people."

"**Teaching assistants often get a bad reputation** here at UT, but many of the best teachers I have had were TAs. They often have a sense of humor and are more laid-back than professors. They seem to identify more with the students and will go the extra mile to teach them something. Others, however, are out to prove themselves and may try to make things difficult."

"Some professors play games with students, which sometimes includes handing out study guide sheets that suggest spending time on things that will not be on the test, requiring expensive books that are rarely or never used, and giving vague answers to questions asked during pre-test classes. **Don't be surprised if they take attendance on days that students like to skip**, such as those right before Spring Break, and they pretty much give out test questions on those days."

The College Prowler Take On... Academics

After the first day of classes, you may feel that UT is a large school with cold and hard professors. As time passes, however, you will learn that they are human and want you to learn the material and develop as a student. Most professors really do want you to visit them during office hours, so don't be afraid to ask for extra help!

Some professors may be difficult to understand, but you will be surprised how easily you pick up on their lingual nuances. Teaching assistants will often make you laugh with clever explanations and witty responses to questions. You will encounter a bad seed from time-to-time, though. Whether it is a professor who is too wrapped up in his research, impossible to understand, or generally lousy at lecturing, chances are strong that you will have no choice but to endure a few bad profs. Every professor has quirks and pet peeves, such as late students, absent students, cell phones, lack of class participation, sleeping, or the mandatory squirming and packing up by students around the class's ending time. *Tennessee 101* is a useful tool to check out professors while scheduling classes. Remember, however, that evaluations are completed by the students that actually show up to class. The expected grades they report and the professor evaluation may be higher than if all students were present.

B-

The College Prowler® Grade on

Academics: B-

A high Academics grade generally indicates that professors are knowledgeable, accessible, and genuinely interested in their students' welfare. Other determining factors include class size, how well professors communicate, and whether or not classes are engaging.

Local Atmosphere

The Lowdown On... Local Atmosphere

Region:
South

City, State:
Knoxville, TN

Setting:
Medium-size college town

Distance from Atlanta:
2 hours

Distance from Nashville:
2 hours

Points of Interest:
Gatlinburg
The Great Smoky Mountains National Park
Pigeon Forge

→

Closest Shopping Malls or Plazas:

Belz Factory Outlet World
(Pigeon Forge, TN)

Knoxville Center Mall

West Town Mall

Closest Movie Theaters:

Regal Cinemas 9
West Town Mall
7600 Kingston Pike
(865) 769-3909

Regal Cinemas Knoxville
Center 10
Knoxville Center Mall
3000 North Mall Rd.
(865) 544-1545

Major Sports Teams:

Predators (hockey)

Titans (football)

City Web Sites

www.knoxville.org

www.cityofknoxville.org

www.knoxvilletennessee.com

Did You Know?

5 Fun Facts about Knoxville:

- The Great Smoky Mountains National Park is **the most visited national park** in the United States.
- Knoxville is considered **a test market for new restaurants**. Many new chains launch in the Knoxville area.
- Knoxville is home to the **Women's Basketball Hall of Fame**.
- Knoxville was home to the **1982 World's Fair**. Attendance was recorded at 11,127,786 visitors.
- Oak Ridge National Laboratories, just a short drive from Knoxville, was the building site of **World War II's atomic bomb**.

Famous People from Knoxville:

James Agee (writer/poet)

Nikki Giovanni (poet)

Dolly Parton (country singer)

Chad Pennington (NFL quarterback)

Quentin Tarantino (film director)

Local Slang:

Knoxville is often pronounced "Nogsvull" by the locals, and referred to as "Knox-Vegas" by many students.

Students Speak Out On... Local Atmosphere

"Knoxville may seem like a big town trapped in a small-town mentality. The people here cling to small-town values and traditions."

"Knoxville—**a drinking town with a football problem**."

"There are **no other campuses in the Knoxville area to party with**. All students at the other schools come here."

"Knoxville is big enough to explore, but **not so big that you will be overwhelmed**. Be sure to go to the Knoxville Museum of Art. We have plenty of concerts downtown and in the Thompson Bowling Arena. You can also check the free *Metro Pulse* newspaper for stuff going on around town."

"Knoxville is **a city highly influenced by college football**. If you are not a football fan, or you despise the color orange, you will be very unhappy being in Knoxville, during football season or not. Except for houses, orange is a highly-accepted color for most everything here."

"If you are from a larger city such as Nashville, Memphis, Atlanta, or Cincinnati, you will probably find Knoxville rather quaint and harmless. **Knoxville does have a small ghetto, but most UT students never see it**. There is no reason to go there unless . . . there is no reason to go there. Everything you could possibly need is in the opposite direction of town."

"**Knoxville might seem really boring if you come from a big city**. We get a few good concerts in every year, and the Women's Basketball Hall of Fame is here. Knoxville is very laid-back. Pellissippi State Technical Community College is the only other large college around here—it's a good school with smaller classes and cheaper prices than UT."

"Knoxville is big enough that **you can find whatever type of activity or people you want**. If you want to party till 5 a.m., you can—UT was rated the number one party school in the nation several years ago. If you'd rather study or get involved with student government or religious groups, you can do that here, too. UT offers just about everything you could look for, and even though it doesn't have a beach really close, there are plenty of cool outdoor activities to do. You can ski or snowboard up in Gatlinburg, which is around 45 minutes away, or head to North Carolina, about two hours away."

"**Knoxville is a great city**. The campus is a major part of the city, but they have a historic downtown and two decent malls. You can always find something to do, and you are only 30 minutes away from the SmokyMountains."

"If you were standing atop a medium-tall building, you could look and see very beautiful houses alongside the river. Turn your head and you would see an old industrial region that resembles a World War II bomb run. **Certain parts of Knoxville have been very well taken care of**, while others look completely trashed."

"I love the atmosphere at UT. **The people there are so cool, especially around football season**. There are other colleges in Knoxville, but they aren't big at all, and a lot of the people that go there are people that failed out of UT. There are places to visit around Knoxville, so when you want to get away, you can."

"The atmosphere of the town is a case of two extremes. **When things are going on, this town is so exciting**. When things are not going on, this place is like the weather—dull and gray. They are no other universities in the same town. You should visit events that go on in the downtown area, but other than that, you are visiting each other in the dorms or apartments."

"**Knoxville is a nice little city**. My hometown has more people than Knoxville, and I think more people live on Long Island than the entire state of Tennessee, so most things are quite different for me here. I like the change, though. It's more relaxed, and there isn't much pressure. The school isn't that expensive, either."

"I highly recommend UT. Knoxville is a medium-sized town, and despite what some may say, there's plenty to do. **We have more restaurants per capita than any other city**, and the nightlife is very diverse. You couldn't pick a school with more spirit than UT."

The College Prowler Take On...
Local Atmosphere

Knoxville truly serves as a happy medium between a large city and a small town. It is an easy transition for students coming from either extreme. In a way, Knoxville can be as large as you want it to be, depending on how willing you are to travel and explore.

The people of Knoxville are rather relaxed (except on game day), and there are plenty of places to go to enjoy leisurely activities. You will not feel trapped in Knoxville. Atlanta and Nashville are not too far away, and you can be in the mountains in even less time. While many consider Knoxville a "college town," not all of the exciting activities take place on campus. You may find that Knoxville is the ideal size for a college student.

B

The College Prowler® Grade on

Local Atmosphere: B

A high Local Atmosphere grade indicates that the area surrounding campus is safe and scenic. Other factors include nearby attractions, proximity to other schools, and the town's attitude toward students.

Safety & Security

The Lowdown On... Safety & Security

Number of UT Police:
50 officers

UT Police Phone:
(865) 974-3114, or 4-3114 from an on-campus phone

Safety Services:
Blue-light phones
Multiple van services
Security in select buildings

Health Services:
Basic medical services
Children's research hospital
Level I trauma center

Health Center Office Hours:
Monday–Friday
8 a.m.–4:30 p.m.

Did You Know?

Eight full-time physicians, one full-time psychiatrist, and 13 full-time nurses **work at the health center**, and all are board certified.

Students Speak Out On...
Safety & Security

"It seems that there are always cops cruising the streets, no matter the time of day. You almost can't walk across campus without seeing a police car."

"**Security on campus is at a medium level**, not to loose and not strict. You feel safe in some places, and in others, you feel threatened. Safety is just the same as security; the University tries to put on a good front, but sometimes, events happen that soil that front."

"I think that **the University is really safe**, all things considered. The campus has a van service that runs a basic route around the campus at night, so you never have to walk alone. There's also an escort service. You can call and tell them your exact location, and they will pick you up or take you somewhere, depending on your distance from campus. The campus has more than 50 blue-emergency phones located at various places around campus. The phones have buttons that will contact the police. UT has its own police station and real police, not just campus cops."

"As with all schools, **crimes on campus do happen**. If you're smart and don't go out late by yourself, though, you should be fine. Campus security offers a number of great services like shuttles to dorms and around campus at night, emergency-call boxes around campus, and free self-defense courses."

"**UT has a new late-night van service**. My experience has been that it responds very quickly, usually in two to three minutes. There is a lot of room on the large buses to accommodate your friends, as well."

"The **campus is about as safe as you make it**. Use common sense and follow a few simple rules, and you will never be in danger. Avoid dark places where no other people are present. As soon as you arrive on campus, write down the van service number and put it in your pocket or save it in your cell phone. You never know when you'll need a ride."

"For the most part, it is safe as long as you use your head. **Don't go out at night alone**, avoid certain areas like Tom Black track after dark, and use good sense. There is at least one rape every semester, and sometimes more, though I have never heard of them catching a rapist. That doesn't mean that they don't, it just means I that have never heard about it. There are security phones all over campus, so if you get in trouble, you can find one of the blue-light phones and automatically call the UTPD. UT provides shuttle vans for students at night so that no one has to walk from the library to their dorm in the dark. Most pathways are well lit, and you must be escorted by a dorm resident in order to get in the dorm's door. All dorm residents have keys to the dorm they live in and the access doors remained locked at all times."

"Police are usually present on hot spots across campus on the weekends. They will drive through Fraternity Park every 10 minutes or so, and they patrol the strip both in cars and on foot. **There are also several officers that patrol on bicycles**. It seems the overall presence of the police has greatly increased in the three years I have been here."

"**Cops can be pretty strict at times**. They will pull you over for even the smallest traffic violation. Watch out for one-way streets! Be warned, though, they check your speed on Volunteer Boulevard with radar. Don't speed on campus!"

"**Security is pretty tight in the dorms**. Your student ID card, which is coded and has your picture on it, gets you into your dorm and accesses your meal plan on campus."

"There have been a few bad incidents over the last few years that got a lot of local media coverage, but many of them occurred in places most students never go. In general, the **UTPD does an excellent job and will make you feel safe**."

"**There are always cops out patrolling** and UT has its own police department, which is nice. The only problems occur when people are stupid and walk alone late at night, or something like that. Even then, there aren't many incidents, and I feel very safe."

The College Prowler Take On... Safety & Security

Most students' opinions on safety and security boil down to one thing—using your common sense. Even with all of the services the UTPD offers, none are a replacement for using your head. The UTPD take their jobs very seriously and are always looking out for students' safety. For a school of UT's size, they are very successful, and the majority of students don't walk around with spray-mace key rings tightly in hand.

All of the services mentioned here are at your disposal and are sure to make you feel safer. Make sure you know the numbers to call if need be, and if you don't already have one, a cell phone may be a good investment (sorry, mom and dad). By programming them into your cell phone on your day of arrival, you may dodge a few uncomfortable moments.

B

The College Prowler® Grade on

Safety & Security: B

A high grade in Safety & Security means that students generally feel safe, campus police are visible, blue-light phones and escort services are readily available, and safety precautions are not overly necessary.

Computers

The Lowdown On... Computers

High-Speed Network?
Yes

Wireless Network?
Yes

Number of Labs:
27

Operating Systems:
Mac OS
UNIX
Windows

Discounted Software

Adobe and Corel programs, Macromedia Flash, Microsoft Office suites, and others are available to students, faculty, and staff at discount prices (usually 65%–75% off retail). For more information, visit *www.academic-software-outlet.com*.

Free Software

Communication Suite, JMP, McAfee AntiVirus, SAS, S-PLUS, SPSS, Maple, Lotus Notes

24-Hour Labs?

No

Charge to Print?

No

Did You Know?

? The University's network is extremely fast! Get ready for some intense **online gaming and file sharing** throughout your dorm!

Students Speak Out On...
Computers

"There's a plethora of labs, you just have to find the right one. The library labs are always crowded, but others around campus are usually easily accessible."

"**The computer network is great—it kicks DSL's butt**! The computer labs aren't usually crowded, though you will find a few people at a number of the computers at any given time. The only time you really have to wait is during test week or during midday class time at the library. Bringing your own computer is a pretty good idea for late-night paper writing and searching the Internet for information. It seems to be more convenient than having to walk to a lab to do work. The labs in Presidential Court close at midnight, so if you have something to do at the last minute, you have to go to the library in the dark. It's an interesting walk alone at night—it's not scary, just interesting."

"**The Ethernet connections are lightning fast**. Most people have probably never used a connection like this, so you will have more music and movies than you can imagine. It slows down slightly in the afternoon when everyone gets back from class, but not a lot. Bring plenty of CDs to burn if you have a burner."

"The dorm rooms have an Internet hookup and run on Ethernet, which is pretty quick. There are a few computer labs around campus. **The library labs are generally busy**, but you can usually get on one if you wait a little bit. I would recommend bringing your own computer, but I know it's not always feasible. If you can't, there are plenty of labs, and you can usually find time to use one of the University computers."

"**One very important tool at this University is AOL Instant Messenger**. It is how everyone communicates, and if you do not have it, you will certainly be out of the loop. You can use it in the labs now because of the quick messenger software on the AOL Web site, which is an added bonus."

"**If you have your own computer, I recommend bringing it**, although our computer labs are very high-tech and up-to-date. There are certain times of day, and of the year, when they are packed, and you have to wait forever to get on a computer. It's just more convenient to have your own PC."

"Even if you do have a PC of your own, **you may want to consider doing all of your printing in the labs**. Since paper is free, aside from angering a few other people waiting to print, you can print out dozens of pages of notes and lecture slides."

"**UT recently put new computers in all the labs**. They are pretty well maintained and have most of the software you would need for classes. There is even a small lab in the cafeteria."

"If you live in a dorm, I strongly suggest that you bring your own computer. My roommate and I both had ours, and it worked out great. There are labs all over the place, but you will use a computer so much that **you will wish that you had one in your room**. We have T1 Internet connections all over campus, and it is very fast. There were a couple of times when it shut down, but never for more than a day or two at a time."

"**The computer network is great**. Everyone on campus is hooked up with T1 connections. UT has a lot of computer labs, so you can usually find one with a free computer, but I recommend bringing your own."

The College Prowler Take On...
Computers

Vast improvements have taken place in the last several years in regards to technology. Computers accessible to students are fairly new, and the network is speedy enough to satisfy those accustomed to DSL and cable networks. No matter how many computers are on campus, nothing beats having a computer of your own. Very few people come to Knoxville without one, and you will probably regret not having a personal computer when the labs are crowded or inconvenient.

UT's computer store, located in the UC, has just about every software application you will need, and most of the hardware you might need, as well. If computers have not been a big part of your life so far, you will be surprised how dependant you become. Downloading music and communicating with friends is only the tip of the iceberg. Many class-related needs can be fulfilled on a computer, and it is commonly a priority to set up your PC the day that you arrive.

B

The College Prowler® Grade on

Computers: B

A high grade in Computers designates that computer labs are available, the computer network is easily accessible, and the campus' computing technology is up-to-date.

Facilities

The Lowdown On... Facilities

Student Center:

The University Center (UC)

Athletic Centers:

The "Bubble"

The HPER Building

The Student Aquatic Center

Libraries:

George F. DeVine Music Library

James D. Hoskins Library

John C. Hodges Main Library

Webster Pendergrass Agricultural-Veterinary Medicine Library

Campus Size:

730 acres

What Is There to Do on Campus?

Grab some food, go out for a coffee or beer depending on your preference and age, take an opportunity to work out, or take in a dollar movie at the UC. Basically, the options are there, it's just a matter of going out and doing it.

Movie Theater on Campus?

Affordable movies are periodically shown in the UC.

Bowling on Campus?

The bottom level of the UC, appropriately called "the Down Under," has bowling for under three dollars, with little or no wait.

Bar on Campus?

No, there are no bars on the campus, per se, but there are many good bars on the strip, such as Cool Beans, Hannah's, Charlie Pepper's, Henry's, Liquid Knoxville, Old College Inn, and Campus Pub.

Coffeehouse on Campus?

There is a Starbucks located in the Hodges Library.

Favorite Things to Do

Play intramural flag football, soccer, softball, ultimate Frisbee, and basketball; swim laps at the Student Aquatic Center pool; and workout at the "Bubble."

Popular Places to Chill

You can chill out by the pool and study (but it is only fair to warn you, it can be a bit distracting on busy days), and watch one of the many intramural games taking place throughout the year. There are also a number of places on the strip to chill, but many are over 21 after a certain time. Hanging out with friends in dorms is also popular.

Students Speak Out On...
Facilities

"The UC has a basement where you can bowl or play pool, air hockey, or Ping Pong. You can even take bowling as a class! I never even learned how to check out a book from our huge Hodge Library until May!"

"The **facilities on campus are in the process of being updated**. The only facility that is current is the athletic facility because it is always being remodeled or updated. The computer labs are fairly updated and are only a couple of years behind the latest models. The student center badly needs renovation to become somewhat modern."

"**They really try to separate the athletes from regular students at UT**. The athletes have one of just about everything to themselves, and what they have is all cutting-edge and modern. Many of the long-overdue renovations to student facilities are now taking place, and they are now worth a visit."

"The facilities are very nice. They just updated everything, so it's great! **UT has the best workout facility in Tennessee, and it's open to all students**. When it's warm, the pool is a great place to go and lay out, study, or swim."

"**They are always building something on campus**. Many of the buildings, however, most students may never set foot in."

"While many of the buildings are new, others are exactly the same as when your mother or father attended UT. All that has been changed in some buildings are the light bulbs, while the desks, flooring, windows, and bathrooms are from the stone age. **Some buildings still have shelters**!"

"My biggest complaint with the older buildings is air conditioning. **There is no rhyme or reason as to when UT turns heating on and off**. During an unusually warm spring semester day, the heat will be blowing at full blast while it's 70 degrees outside. The recently-finished Alumni Memorial Building has a reputation for being frigidly cold year-round. You will be very uncomfortable in either situation, so dress accordingly."

"**We have some of the best facilities in the Southeast**, and we are getting more. Our athletes have the best fitness and study centers around. The computers are all kept up-to-date and are really fast, and the student center is a great place to meet people and catch a bite to eat, or to see a dollar movie."

"**If you run or jog, you should definitely check out Tom Black track**. They resurface it almost every year, and it is smooth and level. It beats jogging across campus, with the uneven sidewalks, traffic, and hills."

"**All the athletic facilities rank among the top in the county**, including the IM facilities. The computer labs have all the necessary equipment for students to complete their studies, and the student center is a decent place to hang out in between classes."

The College Prowler Take On... Facilities

The crème de la crème of facilities is still reserved for athletes. Most students have a mild abhorrence for athletes due to pampering by the University, and feel like athletes are provided with their own large campus "country club." The University does spend a few of the leftover dollars on facilities for students, and most of the students that use them are satisfied with their accessibility and quality.

Most of the academic buildings are rather old, but many have been renovated and brought up to some pretense of modernity. A university of this size suffers a lot of wear and tear. Anything new does not stay new for long, and no matter how hard they try to maintain facilities, some get worn and dirty quickly. While we still do not enjoy marble floors and Italian leather chairs in campus facilities, there have been many improvements over the last several years. UT is eternally a "work in progress," but it is certain athletics will remain top priority.

B+

The College Prowler® Grade on Facilities: B+

A high Facilities grade indicates that the campus is aesthetically pleasing and well-maintained; facilities are state-of-the-art, and libraries are exceptional. Other determining factors include the quality of both athletic and student centers and an abundance of things to do on campus.

Campus Dining

The Lowdown On... Campus Dining

Freshman Meal Plan Requirement?

Yes

Meal Plan Average Cost:

$1,180–$1,380

Places to Grab a Bite with Your Meal Plan:

A&A Café

Food: Grab-n-go

Location: Art and Architecture Building

(A&A Café, continued)

Hours: Monday–Thursday 7:30 a.m.–6 p.m., Friday 7:30 a.m.–5 p.m.

All-American Grill & Grocery

Food: Chick-fil-A, Pizza Hut, Salad Garden, Smokey's Doghouse, Grille Works, Kettle Classics, grocery/convenience

Location: Presidential Court Building

Hours: Grill: Monday–Thursday 10:30 a.m.–12 a.m., Friday–Saturday 10:30 a.m.–10 p.m.

→

→

(All-American Grill & Grocery, continued)

Grocery: Monday–Thursday 11 a.m.–10 p.m., Friday–Saturday 10:30 a.m.–10 p.m.

Andy's Pantry

Food: Convenience, grab-n-go items

Location: Andy Holt Apartments

Hours: Monday–Friday 7:30 a.m.–1 a.m., Saturday–Sunday 10 a.m.–1 a.m.

The Café

Food: American, salad bar, Starbucks coffee

Location: Thompson-Boling Arena

Hours: Monday–Friday 7 a.m.–3 p.m.

Granny Greve Grocery

Food: Convenience, grab-n-go items

Location: Greve Hall

Hours: Monday–Friday 7:30 a.m.–1 a.m., Saturday–Sunday 10 a.m.–1 a.m.

The Hermitage Room

Food: Fine dining

Location: UC top floor

Hours: Monday–Friday 11 a.m.–2 p.m.

Howler's Grill

Food: American, Grille Works

Location: Hess Hall

Hours: Monday–Friday 7:30 a.m.–2:30 p.m.

Mabel's Café

Food: American, Starbucks

Location: McCord Hall

Hours: Monday–Friday 7 a.m.–2 p.m.

Morrill Dining

Food: Restaurant, buffet

Location: Morrill Hall

Hours: Monday–Friday 7 a.m.–10 a.m., 10:30 a.m.–2:30 p.m., 4:30 p.m.–7:30 p.m.

Presidential Court Café

Food: Pan Geos (pasta, mediterranean), buffet

Location: Presidential Courtyard

Hours: Monday–Friday 7 a.m.–10 a.m., 10:30 a.m.–2:30 p.m., 4:30 p.m.–7:30 p.m.; Saturday 8 a.m.–2:30 p.m., 4:30 p.m.–7 p.m.; Sunday 8:30 a.m.–2:30 p.m.

Rocky Top Café

Food: Quiznos, Burger King, Starbucks, Edy's Ice Cream, Miso, Carver Street Market, sushi

Location: University Center

Hours: Monday–Friday 7 a.m.–5 p.m.

The Sidebar Café

Food: Starbucks, grab-n-go items

Location: Taylor Law School Building

Hours: Monday–Friday 7:30 a.m.–2:30 p.m.

→

→

Smokey's

Food: Tortilla Fresca, Tennessee Subs, Woodstone's, The Squeeze, Take One!, It's a Toss Up!, World's Fare, and Smokey's Traditions

Location: University Center

Hours: Monday–Thursday 7 a.m.–2:30 p.m., 4:30 p.m–7:30 p.m.; Friday 7 a.m.–2 p.m.

Smoothie King

Food: Smoothies, sports drinks

Location: Rec Sports Center

Hours: Monday–Thursday 8 a.m.–10 p.m., Friday 8 a.m.–9 p.m. Saturday–Sunday 8 a.m.–7 p.m.

Sophie's Place

Food: Buffet

Location: Strong Hall

Hours: Monday–Friday 7 a.m.–10 a.m., 10 a.m.–2:30 p.m., 4:30 p.m.–7:30 p.m.

The Sweet Tooth

Food: Grocery, grab-n-go items

Location: Presidential Courtyard

Hours: Monday–Friday 7 a.m.–12 a.m., Saturday 10:30 a.m.–12 a.m., Sunday 10:30 a.m.–12 a.m.

Off-Campus Places to Use Your Meal Plan:

Off-Campus Dining Network meal plans are available. These act as debit accounts for use at local restaurants. See *www.ocdn.com* for details.

24-Hour On-Campus Eating?

No

Student Favorites:

Smokey's in the UC for lunch, and breakfast at any of the cafeterias.

Did You Know?

Pay close attention to the meal plan rules. There are only certain hours you can use your daily allowance for meals. Meals not within certain hours are deducted from "bonus bucks." Prices of goods in the small snack shops in and around dorms are highly inflated.

Students Speak Out On...
Campus Dining

"The food on campus is on both sides of the spectrum. The student center is where you can get the best food and Presidential Court is a close second. The other food places are either horrible or average."

"I eat my meals in Gibbs Hall with all the athletes and non-athlete residents who live in Gibbs. **A lot of the football players live in Gibbs**, and since Tennessee cares so much about football, this cafeteria has the best food by far. I'm not sure if non-resident, non-athletes can eat there, though. I ate in the other dining hall last year, and the food was pretty good, though it was what you would expect in a college dining hall."

"As a freshman, **you will love eating the fast food in Presidential**. It is quick and tastes pretty good, but I promise you will miss home cooking after a few weeks. Be forewarned, eating this stuff every day can pack on the pounds!"

"**The food isn't bad**. We have about six dining halls across campus with regular food like steaks, ham, and stuff like that. There's also a Burger King, Quiznos, and Edy's Ice Cream, so there is no need to complain about the food. There are even mini-grocery stores in some of the dorms."

"**Dining in the UC has gotten much better over the last two years**. The food is near restaurant quality with great recipes and variety. As expected, with all the renovation and new offerings, prices have also gone up. You almost can't get a decent, filling meal at the UC for less than six dollars."

"**My best advice for subscribing to a meal plan is keep track of your bonus bucks**! Many freshmen get in the habit of mindlessly scanning their card everyday. Since you will probably use them, even if you don't visit snack shops, they go pretty quickly. Since cigarettes can be purchased with bonus bucks, some freshmen take up smoking and spend them rapidly. If you choose to smoke, don't buy your cigarettes at snack shops. Walk to the strip and buy a carton, it may save you $10–$15."

"I think that the food on campus is pretty decent. There are a variety of cafeterias located around campus with buffet-style food. If I remember correctly, every cafeteria has a salad bar and a sandwich bar, and one section that offers food made to your preference, like pasta or sandwich wraps. **There is always a vegetarian option, too, if that is something you need**. There are cafeterias that resemble mini-food courts, with options like Chick-fil-A, Pizza Hut, Burger King, Edy's Ice Cream, sub sandwiches, home-cooked food, and Starbucks. You just need to make sure that you look at the different meal plan options to ensure that you get what you want. There are also bonus bucks, which are great and act like a debit card on your student ID. The bonus bucks allow you to shop at some of the on-campus grocery stores and eat over your daily allowance."

"If there are certain snacks that you cannot live without, bring as many as you can to school with you. While you can eat meals on the meal plan, **all snacks are deducted from bonus bucks**. Also, bring as much soap, shaving supplies, deodorant, and toiletries as you can. Those are among the highest priced items in the small shops, and there is hardly any variety. Don't plan on finding your usual brand of shampoo."

"Most people will complain about cafeteria slop or whatever, but I don't think the food is bad for the mass-produced type that you find in any school's cafeteria. **It's warm and fresh, and there is a varied menu** so you don't eat the same old thing all the time. We also have what is called "the Grill," where you can get Chick-fil-A or Pizza Hut, among other things. Salad bars are provided everywhere, as are dessert bars, if that is your thing."

"The food is yummy—**there are tons of fast-food places** to eat and campus food is decent. There are four all-you-can-eat cafeterias, three of which are usually the same. The other one, the Varsity Inn, is in the dorm where the football players live, and the food there is excellent. You have to have a special meal plan or use a different form of payment to eat there, though—it's not included with the regular meal plans. There are also two pay-as-you-go places. One includes places like Pizza Hut, Chick-fil-A, a sub shop, a burger bar, and salads. The other, Smokey's, is a lot like the other cafeteria food, but better. If you can stand to eat fast food everyday, eat at the All-American Grill or at Smokey's—the food is far better there."

The College Prowler Take On...
Campus Dining

If you live in a dorm as a freshman, which is required for non-commuters, you are more or less required to purchase a meal plan. Students' opinions vary on the quality and selection of food, but most are satisfied with what UT has offered. When you have had your fill of cafeteria food, there are many fast food options. One thing is for certain, you will gain a whole new appreciation for your mother's cooking that you had taken for granted so many years. You will clean your plate, and possibly the rest of the family's plates, during each visit.

Since you will be stuck with the UT Dining Services meal plan, why not make the most of it? The key is to read and understand the meal plan rules. Keep track of your bonus bucks, and eat during allotted dining hours. If you know you are going to need something, such as snacks, and have room to pack them, stock up as much as possible! Finally, remember that bonus bucks do not roll over. If you have $200 left at the end of the semester, it will not be added to the following semester. Take my word for it, the money is not donated to charity and is not tax deductible, so if you don't use it, you have essentially thrown it away.

B

The College Prowler® Grade on

Campus Dining: B

Our grade on Campus Dining addresses the quality of both school-owned dining halls and independent on-campus restaurants as well as the price, availability, and variety of food.

Off-Campus Dining

The Lowdown On... Off-Campus Dining

Restaurant Prowler: Popular Places to Eat!

Buffalo Wild Wings
Food: Wings
1912 Cumberland Ave.
(865) 524-9464
Price: $15 and under
Hours: Monday–Thursday 11 a.m.–1 a.m., Friday–Saturday 11 a.m.–2 a.m., Sunday 12 p.m.–12 a.m.

Calhoun's on the River
Food: American
400 Neyland Dr.
(865) 673-3355
Price: $15 and under
Hours: Monday–Friday 11 a.m.–10 p.m., Saturday 11 a.m.–11 p.m., Sunday 11 a.m.–9:30 p.m.

The Copper Cellar
Food: American
1807 Cumberland Ave.
(865) 673-3411
Price: $20 and under

→

(The Copper Cellar, continued)

Hours: Monday–Thursday 5 p.m.–10 p.m., Friday–Saturday 5 p.m.–11 p.m.

Cracker Barrel

Food: Traditional

5001 Central Ave. Pike

(865) 688-7396

www.crackerbarrel.com

Price: $15 and under

Hours: Sunday–Thursday 6 a.m.–10 p.m., Friday–Saturday 6 a.m.–11 p.m.

Don Pablo's

Food: Mexican

2904 East Towne Mall Circle

(865) 633-4978

www.donpablos.com

Price: $15 and under

Hours: Sunday–Thursday 11 a.m.–10 p.m., Friday–Saturday 11 a.m.–11 p.m.

Green Hills Grille

Food: American

4429 Kingston Pike

(865) 558-0091

www.greenhillsgrille.com

Price: $15 and under

Hours: Sunday 10 a.m.–10 p.m., Monday–Thursday 11 a.m.–10 p.m., Friday–Saturday 11 a.m.–11 p.m.

Hooters of Knoxville

Food: American

8050 Kingston Pike

(865) 694-4668

www.hooters.com

Price: $10 and under

Hours: Monday–Thursday 11 a.m.–12 a.m., Friday–Saturday 11 a.m.–1 a.m., Sunday 12 p.m.–11 p.m.

IHOP

Food: Pancakes

7128 Kingston Pike

(865) 588-8331

www.ihop.com

Price: $10 and under

Hours: Daily 24 hours

Kanpai of Tokyo

Food: Japanese

1645-A Downtown West Blvd.

(865) 693-3903

www.kanpaioftokyo.com

Price: $15 and under

Hours: Monday–Thursday 11:30 a.m.–2 p.m., 5 p.m.–9:30 p.m.; Friday 11:30 a.m.–2 p.m., 5 p.m.–9:30; Saturday 11:30 a.m.–2 p.m., 5 p.m.–10 p.m.; Sunday 12 p.m.–2:30 p.m., 5 p.m.–8:30 p.m.

Krystal Restaurant

Food: American

2800 E Magnolia Ave.

(865) 524-9975

Price: $10 and under

(Krystal Restaurant, continued)

Hours: Daily 24 hours

Litton's Market and Restaurant

Food: American

2803 Essary Dr.

(865) 688-0429

Price: $10 and under

Hours: Monday–Thursday 11 a.m.–8 p.m., Friday–Saturday 11 a.m.–10 p.m.

The Original Louis' Drive-In Restaurant

Food: American

4661 Old Broadway

(865) 688-4121

Price: $10 and under

Hours: Tuesday–Sunday 11 a.m.–10 p.m.

Mellow Mushroom

Food: Pizza

2109 Cumberland Ave.

(865) 524-7979

Price: $10 and under

Hours: Monday–Thursday 11 a.m.–11 p.m., Friday–Saturday 11 a.m.–12 a.m., Sunday 12 p.m.-10 p.m.

The Melting Pot

Food: Steak and lobster

111 North Central St.

(865) 971-5400

www.meltingpot.com

(The Melting Pot, continued)

Price: $40 and under

Hours: Sunday–Thursday 5 p.m.–9 p.m., Friday–Saturday 5 p.m.–10 p.m.

O'Charley's

Food: Pub-style

8077 Kingston Pike

(865) 691-5885

www.ocharleys.com

Price: $25 and under

Hours: Monday–Thursday 11 a.m.–11 p.m., Friday–Saturday 11 a.m.–12 a.m., Sunday 10:30 a.m.-9 p.m.; lounge open to 3 a.m. nightly

Olive Garden

Food: Italian

7206 Kingston Pike

(865) 584-7300

www.olivegarden.com

Price: $25 and under

Hours: Sunday—Thursday 11 a.m.–10 p.m., Friday–Saturday 11 a.m.–11 p.m.

Papa John's

Food: Pizza

7000 Kingston Pike

(865) 584-7272

www.papajohns.com

Price: $10 per person

Hours: Daily 11 a.m.–11 p.m.

P.F. Chang's

Food: Chinese

6741 Kingston Pike

(865) 212-5514

Price: $20 and under

Hours: Sunday–Thursday 11 a.m.–11 p.m., Friday–Saturday 11 a.m.–12 a.m.

Puleo's Grille

Food: Southern/Italian

260 N. Peters Rd.

(865) 691-1960

Price: $20 and under

Hours: Sunday–Thursday 11 a.m.–10 p.m., Friday–Saturday 11 a.m.–11 p.m.

Regas

Food: Steakhouse

318 N. Gay St.

(865) 637-3427

www.thechophouse.com/regas_index.html

Price: $25 and under

Hours: Monday–Tuesday 11 a.m.–2:30 p.m., 5 p.m.–9 p.m., Wednesday 11 a.m.–2:30 p.m., 5 p.m.–9:30 p.m., Thursday–Friday 11 a.m.–2:30 p.m., 5 p.m.–10 p.m., Saturday 5 p.m.–10 p.m.

Riverside Tavern

Food: American

950 Volunteer Landing

(865) 637-0303

http://riversidetavern.org/daily.htm

(Riverside Tavern, continued)

Price: $12 and under

Hours: Monday–Thursday 11 a.m.–10 p.m., Friday 11 a.m.–11 p.m., Sunday 11 a.m.–9 p.m.

Steak 'n Shake

Food: Steaks, shakes

310 Wild Geese Rd.

(865) 675-2551

Price: $10 and under

Hours: Daily 24 hours

Subway

Food: Subs

25 Market Square

(865) 524-9446

Price: $10 and under

Hours: Sunday–Friday 9 a.m.–5 p.m., Saturday 9 a.m.–4:30 p.m.

Tennessee Grill

Food: American

900 Neyland Dr.

(865) 862-8657

www.tennesseegrill.com

Price: $15 and under

Hours: Monday–Thursday 11 a.m.–10 p.m., Friday–Saturday 11 a.m.–11 p.m., Sunday 10:30 a.m.–10 p.m.

Ye Olde Steak House

Food: Steak

401 Henley St.

(865) 577-9328

→

(Ye Olde Steakhouse, continued)

Hours: Sunday–Thursday 4:30 p.m.–9 p.m., Friday–Saturday 4:30 p.m.–9:30 p.m.

Other Places to Check Out:

Charlie Pepper's

Panera Bread

Ruby Tuesday

Closest Grocery Store:

Kroger's
4918 Kingston Pike
(865) 584-0201

Late-Night, Half-Price Food Specials:

If you want to keep up to date with what places are offering deals at the moment, look for advertisements in the *Daily Beacon*, UT's campus newspaper.

24-Hour Eating:

IHOP

Krystal

Steak 'n Shake

Best Pizza:

Mellow Mushroom (sit-down)

Papa John's (take-out)

Best Chinese:

P.F. Chang's

Best Italian:

The Original Louis'

Puleo's Grille

Best Japanese:

Kanpai of Tokyo

Best Hamburger:

Litton's Market and Restaurant

Best Steak:

Ye Olde Steak House

Best Breakfast:

Cracker Barrel

Best Wings:

Buffalo Wild Wings

Best Healthy:

Subway

Best Fine Dining:

The Melting Pot

Regas

Best Place to Take Your Parents:

Tennessee Grill

Did You Know?

? Ruby Tuesday, a popular restaurant with locations worldwide, was **first opened on the strip by four UT fraternity brothers**.

Students Speak Out On...
Off-Campus Dining

"There are lots of restaurants on what's called 'the Strip,' a stretch of Cumberland Avenue near campus. There's lots of variety, ranging from Chinese or Japanese to many delis, O'Charley's, Copper Cellar, and Panera Bread."

"**Knoxville might as well be the capital for awesome restaurants**. They're all over the place, everywhere you go. There are a couple on the strip, such as Copper Cellar, O' Charley's, Ruby Tuesday, and Charlie Pepper's. There are also tons of fast food places on the strip. A block or two from campus is an area called 'The Old City,' which used to be downtown Knoxville. Now, it is just a hot spot for college kids, but there's an excellent restaurant there called the Melting Pot."

"**The Strip is convenient to go to from campus, with bars and fast food on it**. It's more popular with freshmen because you can walk there. 'The Old City,' the older part of Knoxville, about a five- to ten-minute drive from campus, has more clubs and nicer places to eat."

"There is a **wide variety of restaurants near campus on Cumberland Avenue**. Everyone calls it 'the Strip.' There are fast food restaurants and sit-down restaurants, and you can walk to it from campus without a problem."

"There are a bunch of restaurants on the strip, and **the school is getting a strip meal plan**. The strip has delis, bars, and places like Wendy's and McDonald's to eat, so you may want to look into it."

"Once you grow tired of campus dining and the Strip, **there are many great restaurants in other parts of Knoxville that are actually pretty close**. If you never leave campus for dinner at least a few times, you are really missing out."

"**Knoxville is blessed with many restaurants** exclusive to Knoxville, such as Calhoun's and Copper Cellar. They have excellent menus and reasonable prices."

"**Ye Olde Steak House is truly an institution** in Knoxville. Even the most discriminating steak connoisseur will enjoy their menu. It is an expensive restaurant, but it is worth every penny. When you order a rare steak, it will come rare, and you can skip the steak sauce."

"Prepare yourself for what will sound like a crass advertisement: **Puleo's Grille was voted 'Knoxville's Best Restaurant' by the *Metro Pulse***. Their menu is one of a kind, from classic Southern favorites to Chinese, Italian, and steaks. You will not be disappointed! I recommend the shrimp and grits."

The College Prowler Take On...
Off-Campus Dining

The strip is a convenient and reasonably priced place to enjoy a meal with friends. They have good variety, reasonable prices, and usually aren't extremely busy. Very few cities of comparable size boast the dining prowess of Knoxville. The restaurant business generally has a 50 percent failure rate, but in Knoxville, restaurant buildings do not stay vacant long. Consequently, there is a great variety that caters to every taste.

Your choices will not be solely of the franchise variety due to the many superb "mom-and-pop" eateries. This all stems from Knoxville's love of good food and great atmosphere paired with a low cost of living. The Strip has much to offer, but when you are ready for something different, branching out will offer much more.

A

The College Prowler® Grade on

Off-Campus Dining: A

A high Off-Campus Dining grade implies that off-campus restaurants are affordable, accessible, and worth visiting. Other factors include the variety of cuisine and the availability of alternative options (vegetarian, vegan, Kosher, etc.).

Campus Housing

The Lowdown On... Campus Housing

Room Types:
Singles
Doubles
Apartments

Best Dorms:
Gibbs
Humes
Reese

Worst Dorms:
Clement
Hess
Melrose

Undergrads Living on Campus:
33%

Number of Dorms:
13

Number of University-Owned Apartments:
3 complexes

→

Dormitories:

Apartments Hall

Floors: 15

Total Occupancy: 1150

Bathrooms: In-room

Coed: By floor

Residents: Upperclassmen

Room Types: Apartment-style

Special Features: Private kitchens and living rooms, laundry room, computer lab, Andy's Pantry

Clement Hall

Floors: 8

Total Occupancy: 703

Bathrooms: In-room

Coed: By wing

Residents: Various

Room Types: Suites

Special Features: Meeting room, sunroof, music room, weight room, courtyard with basketball and volleyball courts

Gibbs Hall

Floors: 5

Total Occupancy: 218

Bathrooms: In-room

Coed: No, all male

Residents: Freshmen, upperclassmen (110 rooms reserved for athletes)

Room Types: Suites

Special Features: Computer lab, laundry room, rec room, air-conditioning, Varsity Inn

Greve Hall

Floors: 7

Total Occupancy: 382

Bathrooms: Shared by floor

Coed: By floor

Residents: Freshmen, upperclassmen (female floors reserved for sorority members)

Room Types: Doubles

Special Features: Weight room, music room with piano, outdoor volleyball court, computer lab, TV/ study lounges, Granny Greve Convenience Store & Deli

Hess Hall

Floors: 6

Total Occupancy: 1026

Bathrooms: Shared by floor

Coed: By wing

Residents: Various

Room Types: Doubles

Special Features: TV lounge, laundry room, exercise equipment, computer lab, Hess Express Grocery & Grill

Humes Hall

Floors: 6

Total Occupancy: 518

Bathrooms: In-room

Coed: No, all female

Residents: Various

Room Types: Suites

Special Features: Exercise room, closed-circuit TV lounge, sunroof, computer lab, air-conditioning, located in Presidential Court complex

Massey Hall

Floors: 8

Total Occupancy: 584

Bathrooms: Shared by floor

Coed: No, all female

Residents: Sorority members

Room Types: Doubles

Special Features: Computer lab, big-screen TV lounge, laundry room

Melrose Hall

Floors: 4

Total Occupancy: 189

Bathrooms: Shared by floor

Coed: In-room

Residents: Overflow

Room Types: Singles

Special Features: Computer lab, laundry room, kitchen, open during breaks

Morrill Hall

Floors: 14

Total Occupancy: 758

Bathrooms: In-room

Coed: By floor

Residents: Various

Room Types: Suites

Special Features: Music room, study room, laundry room, rec room, Morrill Cafeteria on the second floor

North Carrick Hall

Floors: 11

Total Occupancy: 495

Bathrooms: In-room

Coed: No, all male

(North Carrick Hall, continued)

Residents: Freshmen, upperclassmen

Room Types: Suites

Special Features: TV lounge, pool table, Ping Pong, music room, study room, computer lab and air conditioning, located in Presidential Court complex

Reese Hall

Floors: 6

Total Occupancy: 512

Bathrooms: In-room

Coed: No, all male

Residents: Various

Room Types: Suites

Special Features: Weight room, sunroof, laundry room, multipurpose room, computer lab, located in Presidential Court complex

South Carrick Hall

Floors: 11

Total Occupancy: 530

Bathrooms: In-room

Coed: No, all female

Residents: Various

Room Types: Suites

Special Features: TV lounge, sunroof, music room, study room, computer lab and air conditioning, located in Presidential Court complex

Strong Hall

Floors: 4

Total Occupancy: 273

Bathrooms: Communal or in-suite, depending on room

Coed: No, all females

Special Features: Exercise room, study lounges, computer lab, music room, Sophie's Place dining hall

University-Owned Apartments:

Golf Range Apartments

Floors: 420 apartments, two stories each

Total Occupancy: 416 apartments

Bathrooms: Private

Coed: Yes

Residents: Upperclassmen

Room Types: One- and two-bedroom apartments

Special Features: Laundry rooms, maintenance shop, swimming pool, playgrounds, tennis courts, basketball court, computer lab, bus stop

Laurel Apartments

Floors: 14

Total Occupancy: 320 apartments

Bathrooms: Private

Coed: Yes

Residents: Upperclassmen

Room Types: One- and two-bedroom apartments

Special Features: Laundry rooms, swimming pool, playground, rec room, computer lab

Sutherland Apartments

Floors: 13 three-story buildings

Total Occupancy: 420 apartments

Bathrooms: Private

Coed: Yes

Residents: Upperclassmen

Room Types: One-, two-, and three-bedroom apartments

Special Features: Laundry room, rec room, swimming pool, playgrounds, tennis court, basketball court, computer lab

Bed Type

Twin extra-long

Cleaning Service?

The double occupancy rooms have a maid service that performs light cleaning of bathrooms.

What You Get

All residents are provided with cable and computer connections, a desk, desk chair, dresser, closet, mattress pad, trash can, microfridge (combination refrigerator/freezer/microwave), and a telephone with free local calling.

Did You Know?

Gibbs Hall is required by NCAA regulations to house a minimum of 51 percent non-athletes. It is still, however, very difficult for freshman non-athletes to get a room assignment there.

Students Speak Out On... Campus Housing

> **"For a freshman, Humes, South Carrick, and Morrill are all great. Avoid Clement if you aren't into the old-building feel, and know that Humes has the best staff."**

"**The dorms are generally run-down** and need a lot of remodeling to become modern looking and accommodating. The most popular dorms are around the Presidential Court area (Humes, North & South Carrick, and Reese). The dorms to run away from are Clement and Hess. If you like the tight-knit community opportunity, Hess and Morrill are your best bets."

"**The dorms are fairly nice**. Hess is the freshman dorm, and people there are generally crazy, earning it the nickname 'the Zoo'. Other dorms are a little nicer, but nowhere near as fun."

"**Hess is by far the most social dorm**. It seems like whether it's night or day, there is always something going on there. It is also located beside the library and is the closest dorm to most classrooms."

"**Girls who are considering joining a sorority should consider moving into Humes**, which always seems to be Greek dominated. The same is true for guys planning to join a fraternity with Reese, but not as dominant. The RAs in these two dorms are also thought to be the best."

"Two words: Hess Hall! **Whatever you do, don't live in Clement Hall**! It's all the way across campus and isolated—they call it 'No Limit Clement.'"

"**The dorms aren't that bad—they're not luxurious** by any means, but they're cool. I stayed in Clement Hall last year, which wasn't too bad. Hess is probably the worst, with community bathrooms and the smallest rooms, which means the least amount of privacy if you have a boyfriend."

"**The dorms are a lot of fun**! I stayed in Hess, and even though I didn't choose it in my top three preferences, I wouldn't change it for the world. All the dorms are 'nice'—they are small and sometimes have community bathrooms, but that isn't a big deal at all. They keep the bathrooms really clean. Half of the time I felt safe going barefoot."

"**The dorms provide a good experience**. If you like to be more social, try South Carrick or Humes. Morrell is too far away. Hess and Melrose are the closest to classes. It seems like anyone who randomly gets put in any dorm always raves about how it's the best, but I would avoid the ones across the street, like Clement, because they're too far."

"**Hess has a reputation for being a bit loud**, but it is close to the library. When you have studying to do, you can be in the library in a few minutes. Everyone in Hess seems to know everyone, and a lot of people really enjoy living there if they can weather the occasional craziness."

The College Prowler Take On...
Campus Housing

There are positive and negative aspects to each dorm. You must make a decision based upon your preferences and priorities. Your academic and social life will not be solely determined by which dorm you are assigned to, and you will be able to make friends no matter where you go. Make sure you understand the rules and regulations of living in each dorm before you arrive. Some of them are rather strict and may catch you off guard.

The dorms have somewhat improved over the last several years. Air conditioning seemed to be one of the biggest complaints. Many of the dorms have working air-conditioners, as well as new windows now, which will pay off from August until the middle of October. Just because you request a dorm does not mean you will ultimately be assigned to that dorm. Since there is no perfect dorm, and none that can really be a huge pain, try to make the most of whatever situation you have and make new friends.

B-

The College Prowler® Grade on

Campus Housing: B-

A high Campus Housing grade indicates that dorms are clean, well-maintained, and spacious. Other determining factors include variety of dorms, proximity to classes, and social atmosphere.

Off-Campus Housing

The Lowdown On... Off-Campus Housing

Undergrads in Off-Campus Housing:
67%

Average Rent For:
1 BR Apt.: $300–$600
2 BR Apt: $400–$650
3 BR Apt.: $500–$800

Popular Areas:
College Park
Jefferson Commons
Sterling University Heights

Best Time to Look for a Place:
January

Students Speak Out On... Off-Campus Housing

"Knoxville has a variety of apartment options throughout the city. Some are very close, while others will send you through rush-hour traffic."

"**Living off campus is not possible for freshmen**, unless you live with a relative. I think it has to be within a certain distance of campus. Aside from that, off-campus housing is not bad. You can usually find a great place in a student living area off campus for a good price."

"**There are numerous options for students** after their freshmen year. You can live anywhere from 100 feet from campus to nearly 20 miles and commute. Some places are worth the money, but most try to rip you off. You get better deals the further you move away from campus."

"**Most of the apartments closer to campus are just as expensive, but not as nice and clean, as those farther** away. Since the landlords know that they don't have to maintain the facilities as well because students will want to live there for location, they let them slip. If you have a car, don't mind driving, and want something quieter and cleaner, you may have to go further from campus."

"**Off-campus housing is nice**. There are quite a few places to choose from—College Park and Sterling Heights, just to name a couple."

"**There are many housing opportunities off campus**. There are many housing areas in the five-block area in between the University and the highway. There are also apartments in other parts of the community, and many offer bus service directly to campus or near campus."

"**Housing in apartments close to campus is outrageous for what you get**. A small, one-bedroom apartment near campus can cost up to $550 a month, before utilities. There are some places near the main interstates that are nicer and cheaper, though farther out. In case you are interested, here is a Web site of places on and off campus: *www.jeffersoncommons.com*. Any search for apartments in Knoxville, Tennessee will turn up some more places."

"We have an off-campus apartment about 10 minutes away from campus simply because we wanted it that way. **There seem to be about 10,000 apartment complexes around, on and off campus**, simply because of the size of UT."

"If you decide to move out of the dorms after your freshman year, **there are plenty of options for every need**. The problem with some of the complexes closer to campus is the noise from parties."

"It's a college campus, **there are plenty of apartments, town houses, and rental houses everywhere**! Most have very good rates, too, and are no more than five minutes from campus. A trolley runs to and from campus all day at 15-minute intervals from most apartments. It saves you a bundle on gas if you have a car, and you won't have to worry about parking.'"

The College Prowler Take On...
Off-Campus Housing

Most students choose to move off campus after one year of living in the dorms. Luckily, Knoxville provides many different options in terms of price, location, and comfort. In general, it is best to start searching as early as you can. Many of the more popular apartments actually have waiting lists and are difficult for the unprepared to rent from, so be sure to pick up free brochures and apartment guides so you will know the details.

The rules for freshman living arrangements are rather elaborate. Unless you are commuting from a dwelling with a relative, you are required to live in the dorms. Make the best of this by meeting as many people as possible and enjoying your first year. Living in an apartment comes with many responsibilities and expenses, but can be much more enjoyable in later college years.

B+

The College Prowler® Grade on

Off-Campus Housing: B+

A high grade in Off-Campus Housing indicates that apartments are of high quality, close to campus, affordable, and easy to secure.

Diversity

The Lowdown On... Diversity

Native American:
Less than 1%

African American:
8%

Asian American:
3%

Hispanic:
1%

White:
87%

International:
1%

Out-of-State:
13%

Political Activity

College Republicans and College Democrats are two of the main political groups on campus.

Gay Pride

The campus is accepting of its gay and lesbian students, and has groups such as the Gay and Straight Political Network and the Lambda Student Union.

Most Popular Religions

Baptist and Methodist are the most prominent religions.

Economic Status

The students at UT run across the board as far as economic status is concerned. Of course, on a college campus, everyone is going to try and convey the impression that they have a bit of money with more expensive clothes and accessories. The economic diversity on campus, however, is very wide ranging.

Minority Clubs

Black Cultural Programming Club, Association of Black Communicators, NAACP, National Society of Black Engineers

Students Speak Out On... Diversity

"UT seems more diverse in actuality than on paper. Minority students will not feel out of place and will make as many friends as anybody."

"**Knoxville is in eastern Tennessee, which is much more predominantly white** than middle and western Tennessee, but I think the campus is still about 15 percent African American. There are a lot of smaller ethnic groups represented, too."

"**The administration has done much to attract minority students**, from multiple programs to a state-of-the-art Black Cultural Center."

"Diversity is one of the main reasons I wanted to come to UT. I went to an all-white high school and was never exposed to other races, but **now I have friends from all over, and it's awesome**."

"**The campus is not as diverse as the administration would like to be**. There are many cultures represented, but not in many numbers, just small pockets of culture. In terms of race, the campus is not diverse, though we try our best."

"**Things are pretty diverse**. There are lots of different types of people who are into a ton of different things—everything from the water-skiing club to NORML, which is an organization for the legalization of marijuana."

"**We are not a very culturally-diverse campus**, but what diversity we do have is respected. There are many different kinds of programs here to showcase other cultures."

"**The new school president made campus diversity a top priority**. He implemented a new way of attracting minority students to the school, and I think there is already a very diverse crowd here."

"**What's diverse here**? This is the South! It is all 'white-bred' folk with the occasional exchange student to provide what little culture there is here."

"The level of diversity present at UT is much higher than you would expect from a school located in east Tennessee. **Most of those that are part of a minority will, for the most part, feel comfortable on campus**."

The College Prowler Take On...
Diversity

Most students will probably agree that UT is much more diverse than the high school they attended, regardless of their background. Many high schools in Tennessee are rather homogeneous, regardless of their size. While an individual's perception of UT's level of diversity may vary, UT does make many efforts to accommodate minority students and make their college experience rewarding.

UT has attempted to attract more minority students through various programs and offerings. UT attracts a wide array of international students, and chances are very likely that you will share a class with one. While UT's level of diversity may be considered less than ideal by many students, students of all backgrounds are comfortable at UT.

D

The College Prowler® Grade on

Diversity: D

A high grade in Diversity indicates that ethnic minorities and international students have a notable presence on campus and that students of different economic backgrounds, religious beliefs, and sexual preferences are well-represented.

Guys & Girls

The Lowdown On...
Guys & Girls

Men Undergrads:
49%

Women Undergrads:
51%

Birth Control Available?

Yes. The Knox County Health Department offers birth control to students in the form of condoms, birth-control pills, and Depo-Provera shots. For female students who would like pills or the Depo-Provera shot, an appointment and initial exam is required. The initial exam is $137, but is on a sliding scale according to income. Refills are also offered. The Family Planning Clinic is located in the basement of the UT Student Health Services Building. For more information, call (865) 215-5320.

Most Prevalent STDs on Campus

Chlamydia and Gonorrhea

Social Scene

Social interaction is somewhat dependent on football season, but it's very active throughout the year.

Hookups or Relationships?

Hookups are slightly more prominent, but if you're looking for a relationship, you can find others that are like-minded, at least in the realm of upperclassmen.

Best Place to Meet Guys/Girls

The Strip, fraternity/sorority events, football games

Did You Know?

Top Three Places to Find Hotties:

1. Bars on the Strip
2. Greek events
3. Exercise facilities

Dress Code

Popular brands/stores from which the UT social-dress code is derived:

Girls – Banana Republic, J Crew, Express, Ann Taylor, North Face, Kate Spade

Guys – Polo, Brooks Brothers, Lacoste, North Face, New Balance

Students Speak Out On...
Guys & Girls

"If you are a guy that prefers the blond-haired, blue-eyed, classy, and posh Southern Belle, UT could be considered their capital. You will not be disappointed."

"You have your hot ones, and you have your not so hot ones, but **they are all pretty good**. Some girls are rather intimidating at first, but most are just afraid of what the other girls they see are thinking about them, and sometimes, guys act the same way."

"Honestly, **we have one of the best-looking campuses** around! Everyone is classy, too. You don't have little hoochie girls walking around without any clothes on. Most everybody dresses in nice-looking, preppy, name-brand clothing."

"**The guys are generally in between a slow-paced or a fast-paced kind of individual**. The slow-paced, non-goal-driven guys generally do very little, including their school work. The fast-paced, goal-driven guys generally have a great grasp on what happens on campus, school, and social life. The girls are also the same way, although there are more fast-paced (goal-driven) girls than there are guys. Most of the girls on this campus are hot, some are hotter than others, and then there are some that generally don't care about being seen, period."

"Gorgeous girls and attractive guys are a dime a dozen here. The only thing that really determines their date-ability is their attitudes. **Many of them know they've got 'it' and act like it**."

"**There are all kinds of people on campus**, but the largest group is the Southerners. It was a nice change to come down South and talk to genuinely nice people. You'll catch the accent, I guarantee it. There are tons of hot guys!"

"If you are from another part of the country that doesn't practice chivalry, you better learn as quickly as possible. Women here will expect doors to be held and chairs to be pulled. **If you cannot learn to be a gentleman, you will be at a great social disadvantage**."

"Girls who prefer the athletic type of guy who takes care of himself and is into playing sports will be very happy here. **Jocks who work out a lot are not hard to find**."

"Compared to students of other college campuses, **the average UT student has more advanced social skills**. UT students pride themselves on their ability to have a good time and interact with those of the opposite sex."

"**Many girls at UT take great pride and spend endless dollars to develop their looks**. If you are a guy and do not take care of yourself, and show only a moderate fashion sense, you will probably be ignored. The way that you dress and carry yourself has great importance. Confidence matters a lot."

"Since UT has so many things that guys love, such as sports and nature, **the selection of guys with many interests is very wide**. Most guys here are very laid-back and friendly. The ones who are jerks and snobs are pretty obvious, and easily avoidable."

"In my many years of being a UT student, **I have never heard anyone complain** about meeting members of the opposite sex. There are guys and girls for every taste, and they are typically very outgoing."

The College Prowler Take On...
Guys & Girls

A walk around campus on a warm September afternoon says it all. Unless you remain confined within dorm walls, you will meet more members of the opposite sex than you could ever hope to remember. Don't worry, though, you'll remember the important ones! Your selection is extremely wide. If a particular guy or girl makes you yawn—next!

Great looks, a fancy car, and impeccable clothing do not always guarantee success with the opposite sex at UT. The common denominator among those truly successful with the opposite sex is a positive attitude and confidence. The outside appearance will only get you so far, especially if you are in it for more than mere casual encounters. In conclusion, there is a huge amount of different types of guys and girls to choose from. Whether you seek a friend, a date, a hookup, or a relationship, there are unlimited choices. You will enjoy meeting the friendly and laid-back students of UT.

A-

The College Prowler® Grade on

Guys: A-

A high grade for Guys indicates that the male population on campus is attractive, smart, friendly, and engaging, and that the school has a decent ratio of guys to girls.

A

The College Prowler® Grade on

Girls: A

A high grade for Girls not only implies that the women on campus are attractive, smart, friendly, and engaging, but also that there is a fair ratio of girls to guys.

Athletics

The Lowdown On... Athletics

Athletic Division:
NCAA Division I
Football Division I-A

Conference:
SEC

School Mascot:
Smokey, a bluetick coonhound

Males Playing Varsity Sports:
235 (3%)

Females Playing Varsity Sports:
148 (2%)

→

Men's Varsity Sports:

Baseball
Basketball
Cross-Country
Football
Golf
Swimming & Diving
Tennis
Track & Field

Women's Varsity Sports:

Basketball
Cheerleading
Cross-Country
Golf
Rowing
Soccer
Softball
Swimming & Diving
Tennis
Track & Field
Volleyball

Club Sports:

Canoe & Hiking
Equestrian
Fencing
Ice Hockey
Lacrosse (Men's and Women's)
Martial Arts
Racquetball
Rowing
Rugby (Men's and Women's)
Sailing
Scuba

(Club Sports, continued)

Ski & Snowboard Club
Soccer (Men's and Women's)
Swimming
Tennis
Tumbling
Ultimate Frisbee (Men's and Women's)
Volleyball (Men's and Women's)
Water Polo
Water Ski

Intramurals:

3 Point Shoot-Out
4-on-4 Flag Football
Basketball
Billiards
Bowling
Buzzball Super Hoops
Flag Football
Floor Hockey
Free Throw
Golf
Punt, Pass, and Kick
Red Zone Challenge
Sand Volleyball
Soccer
Softball
Spring Golf
Table Tennis
Team Tennis
Tennis
Ultimate Frisbee
Volleyball
Wallyball
Wiffleball

Athletic Fields

Lindsey Nelson Baseball Stadium, Fulton Bottoms Field, Intramural Fields, Neyland Stadium, Soccer Complex, and the Softball Stadium

Getting Tickets

The ticket office will announce a weekly schedule where students can scan for tickets. Ticket fees are included in their UT bill as an "activity fee." If you wait until the last minute, you will most likely be issued a "standing-room-only" ticket. Note, students rarely sit in assigned seats, so get to the game early.

Most Popular Sports

On the varsity level, football is the most popular sport by far, but women's basketball is also very popular with the UT crowd. As far as intramurals are concerned, you can find people that are interested in everything.

Overlooked Teams

The men's baseball team does consistently well, but they definitely walk in the shadow of the more popular sports.

Best Place to Take a Walk

Down the strip, across campus on a quiet weekend morning, or nearby Lakeshore Park

Gyms/Facilities

Aquatic Center

The Aquatic Center is one of the finest facilities in college sports, housing an outdoor and indoor Olympic-sized pool. The Aquatic Center has been home to many Olympic training events, and is equipped with a Daktronics timing system that can provide micro-second accuracy for competition. The indoor facility seats approximately 2,000. The Aquatic Center also contains spacious dressing rooms, as well as a weight room featuring Nautilius equiptment.

Neyland-Thompson Sports Complex

The two-level facility includes a 70-yard, All-Pro football field, baseball infield with inlaid bases and a pitcher's mound, as well as housing the Percy Strength Facility and the Tim Kerrin Training Room. The complex is also equipped with dressing facilities, showers, a steam room, suana, equipment distribution center, and locker storage center.

Neyland Stadium

Ranked the #1 college football stadium by *Sporting News* in 2001, the Neyland stadium can seat up to 104,079 fans at any given time. The stadium is one of the most prized facilities at UT.

Thompson-Boling Arena

Seating 24,535, the Thompson-Boling Arena is home to UT basketball. The stadium also has spacious dressing rooms, press work areas, and storage rooms.

Tom Black Track

An eight-lane, Olympic-style oval with dual sets of runways for jumping and pole vaulting. The track can also handle the steeplechase, javelin, and hammer throw events. The track also boasts a state-of-the-art timing system, as well as lights for night meets. Seating for Tom Black track is approximately 7,500+.

Varsity Tennis Courts

The Varsity Tennis Courts consists of six tennis courts and is considered to be one of the finest tennis complexes in the country. There are lights on each court to allow play during the night. The facility also includes a 2,000-seat grandstand and a clubhouse that contains team locker rooms, coaches offices, a press room, press facilities, and a concession stand.

Students Speak Out On...
Athletics

"Everybody in Tennessee is a dedicated Tennessee football fan. I don't think there's a school around that can muster up a better crowd than our 107,000 screaming fans."

"The intensity you will experience at a classic Tennessee football game is incredible. **It is almost like a European soccer match**, except without all the violence."

"**You will know when it is football time in Tennessee**. The tailgaters start showing up mid-week, and the campus will be packed way before the game starts. You will wake up to the sound of the Pride of the Southland Band practicing across the street from the dorms, and you will almost smell the barbecue and Jack Daniels whiskey as soon as you set foot outside. I guarantee that you have never seen so much orange in your life."

"**Varsity sports are a huge part of this campus**. We live and experience every twist and turn of most of the sports teams. IM sports are moderate—football, soccer, basketball, ultimate Frisbee, softball, and golf are the huge sports. There are also club teams and other various sports that you can join."

"**The campus is really active in the fall**, with football games and basketball games. I mean, it is UT football—no explanation should be needed for that. Everyone looks forward to football season because it's so much fun! Going to a UT football game is an experience in itself."

"**Sports at UT are really big**, especially football. Students get free tickets to athletic events, and if you are living on campus, it's an easy walk. IM sports are also pretty big. We have just about every sport imaginable."

"As much as some UT students bellyache about how the athletes get special treatment, the football experience makes it more bearable. **You will love UT during football season**, and even if you aren't that big of a football fan, you will miss it when it is not football season. You will begin counting down the days until the next home game in January."

"**Football is high and mighty, with basketball as the next best**, and we get in to all the home games for free! IM sports are huge if you are Greek, but it's easy to get involved—even if you're not, just round up your dorm floor or friends who want to start a team."

"There are students that never miss out on a football game, home or away. **While some of the away games are a bit of a drive, they can be great road trips**. They are also a great chance to experience other campuses, and if you are in a fraternity or sorority, you can visit your chapter at their campus."

"**IM sports are gaining popularity**, and lots of people are involved in them. Sports are huge on campus. Most people who come to UT come because of the football team. UT football is a way of life in Tennessee. We were the national champions in '98, and everyone pretty much went nuts after that. There are people who live in Knoxville that would sell their first born child for UT football tickets. I am not exaggerating. The two big sports are UT football and women's basketball. They are two of the best teams in the nation."

"**Football is awesome**. We have the second biggest football stadium in the country, and I am sure that if you are interested in watching sports, UT is 10 times better than any other school you could choose. The Lady Vols (women's basketball) are always one of the top two or three teams in the country with a powerhouse team, and we have numerous NCAA and Southeastern Conference indoor titles and an NCAA Mideast Regional title outdoors. In men's sports, we have great baseball and tennis teams, as well. I could keep going! Intramural sports are popular—it is just something to do, though. It isn't anything that you hear about much."

"Varsity sports are huge at UT, ever since we were the national champions in football. UT football is one of the biggest things in Tennessee. Football game days are the bomb. **There are about 150,000 people swarming campus and the strip**, and if you are working as a server on that day, you will make at least $200. Football games are so much fun! I strongly encourage you to go to football games. I even went to a couple of away games last year, like the SEC championship in Atlanta!"

The College Prowler Take On...
Athletics

If you hail from Tennessee, you may be aware of the Vol craze, but you have only heard and seen a small part of what UT athletics is about. If you are from out-of-state, even in an area with a collegiate football team, you will still be surprised by how seriously the Volunteers take football. Even if you are not a huge sports fan, you will enjoy the excitement and tradition that goes along with a football game. It is only fair to warn you that if you dislike sports, you may want to vacate Knoxville in the event of a football game. You will probably have to go pretty far away, though.

IM sports are popular to both play in and watch. There are great chances to play sports, whether it is something you participated in during high school, you want to make friends, or have always wanted to learn. Some sports, such as flag football, are rather competitive. If you played high school varsity sports locally, chances are you might play with or against former high school rivals. A lot of teams go all out, planning practices and purchasing uniforms. In many IM sports, the playoffs draw a pretty big crowd, so you may have an audience when you score or when you drop the ball.

A+

The College Prowler® Grade on
Athletics: A+

A high grade in Athletics indicates that students have school spirit, that sports programs are respected, that games are well-attended, and that intramurals are a prominent part of student life.

Nightlife

The Lowdown On... Nightlife

Club and Bar Prowler: Popular Nightlife Spots!

Club Crawler:

Cotton Eyed Joe

11220 Outlet Dr.

(865) 675-4563

www.cottoneyedjoe.com

A nightclub catering to urban cowboys, Cotton Eyed Joe's music selection is suited to fans of two-step, as well as top 40 hits. They also have pool, darts, an in-house roping ring, and a mechanical bull if dancing's not your thing. There is a loose dress code policy, meaning guys will have to tuck in their shirts, but don't expect the same propriety from the ladies. There are 18-and-over nights, too, and no cover till 7 p.m.

Fiction@125

125 E. Jackson Ave.

(865) 544-4300

www.fictionfx.com

→

(Fiction@125, continued)

Knoxville's premier dance club featuring the best DJs in Tennessee. The club is split into five separate areas, including a courtyard under the stairs, a restaurant, a game room, a frozen daquiri cabana bar, and a VIP room with a private martini bar that overlooks the dancefloor.

Liquid Knoxville

1820 Cumberland Ave.

(865) 329-0411

www.liquidknoxville.com

This is your standard nightclub—a trendy atmosphere, DJs spinning a mix of '80s, '90s, and contemporary hits, a wild dance floor filled with scantily-clad coeds. Monday is College Night and ladies 21 and over get in for free. Cover is generally $5 for 21 and over, and $8 for 18 and over.

Bar Prowler:

Most restaurants on the Strip are equipped with bars, with a few stand-alone bars that serve mostly alcohol, and a limited menu.

Buffalo Wild Wings

1912 Cumberland Ave.

(865) 524-9464

www.buffalowildwings.com

Most people have probably heard of Buffalo Wild Wings by now. For those who haven't, it's a sports bar and restaurant with a great casual atmosphere, plenty of big screen TVs, and a wide and pretty tasty selection of wings.

Charlie Pepper's

716 20th St.

(865) 524-8669

www.charliepeppers.com

Charlie Pepper's is unique to Tennessee, so make sure and check out their original Southwestern-style menu while you stop by for happy hour (4 p.m.–7 p.m. daily). It's a casual spot to have a few drinks with your friends, and there's also the occasional live act, too.

Cool Beans

1817 Lake Ave.

(865) 522-6417

Cool Beans is UT's unofficial "Greek bar," and the members of frats and sororities usually congregate here. They host Greek parties occasionally, and the juke box is packed with pop and top 40 fare.

New Amsterdam Bar & Grill

1836 Cumberland Ave.

(865) 544-7080

Formerly known as RT's Warehouse, the New Amsterdam is a mid-level music venue featuring live acts from several local and national bands such as Superdrag and Mic Harrison.

O'Charley's

1915 Cumberland Ave.

(865) 691-5885

www.ocharleys.com

O'Charley's is known primarily as a popular Southern casual-dining chain, but this franchise on the Strip has transformed itself into a full-time sports bar. The menu is still the same, but expect a different atmosphere from the typical O'Charley's restaurant. A great spot to hit up during happy hour. They occasionally feature live music, as well.

What to Do if You're Not 21

Attend parties on Fraternity Row, "the Fort," or nearby apartments.

Frats

See the Greek section!

Student Favorites:

Buffalo Wild Wings

Charlie Pepper's

Cool Beans

Liquid Knoxville

New Amsterdam Bar & Grill

O'Charley's

Other Places to Check Out:

Banana Joe's

Barley's Taproom & Pizzeria

Boiler Room

Lord Lindsey Mansion

Trio's

Bars Close At:

Most bars close at 3 a.m., with last call at 2:30 a.m.

Useful Resources For Nightlife:

The *Daily Beacon*

The *Knoxville News-Sentinel* weekends section

The *Metro Pulse*

Move Magazine

VOX

Primary Areas with Nightlife:

The Old City

The Strip

Cheapest Place to Get a Drink:

Most bars periodically run specials, depending on the day of the week.

Favorite Drinking Games:

Beer Pong

Century Club

Power Hour

Students Speak Out On...
Nightlife

"Going out can get expensive. Drinks are around $4.50, and pitchers are around $5. It really adds up, especially if you start a tab."

"**As the number one party school in the nation**, UT is surrounded by packed bars from Wednesday through Saturday, especially during the fall semester and football season. O'Charley's and Charlie Pepper's are both excellent choices to get the night started."

"Considering that I am underage, I don't (officially) partake of the bar scene, but I can give you advice about clubs. **Fiction is one of the best in the 'Old City'**—better than any that I have experienced or even heard about from my friends."

"**Barley's in the Old City is a pretty popular place to drink**, and they have live bands every night. Fiction and Lord Lindsey's are popular clubs if you like to dance. Cool Beans, close to the strip, is a popular bar for drinking and hanging out. The men's rugby team hangs out there pretty frequently. They're starting to crack down a lot more on underage drinking than they used to, particularly on the strip."

"**My favorite bar on the strip is Cool Beans**. If you are Greek, this is the place to be. It seems like every fraternity and sorority is represented at this bar on a weekend night. It is pretty easy to walk there, but if you drive, be careful. If you park in the pay lot beside the building, you will get towed lickety-split."

"Let me lay out the week for you—Mondays are tough. **Not a lot of people go out on Mondays, but I'm sure there will be a few people wherever you go**. Tuesdays are best at Buffalo Wild Wings, where they run 30-cent wing specials, so there are usually a few people there hanging out and having a few drinks. Wednesdays, you can head to Trio's, a little pizza place and bar between Hess and Clement Halls. It's usually packed. Thursdays, I sometimes visit the campus pub, but that place gets old kind of quickly. Fridays are rocking anywhere you go. Saturdays are a great time for clubbing, but most clubs are 21 and over on Saturdays, and Knoxville is pretty good at spotting a fake."

"There are four or five good bars on campus on the strip, including Buffalo Wild Wings, O'Charley's which is always hopping during football season, and Charlie Pepper's. Off campus, there is a club called Cotton Eyed Joe's, about 20 minutes from the Strip. It is a country and western line-dancing club, but everybody goes there, not just hicks. **In the Old City, five minutes from campus, there are a bunch of places to party**. One of my favorite clubs is down there is called Fiction. They play techno and dance music. Fiction has two full bars and a great atmosphere. It opens at 10 p.m. and closes at 3 a.m. When Fiction closes, another club called the Boiler Room opens. I've never gone, but I've heard it is cool if you have the stamina for it! There is also a club called Banana Joe's that plays more top 40 music. There are also a few good places to go hear blues and jazz, if you are into that."

"While you may have never have heard of any of the bands, **be sure to check out some of the local music**. Some really great bands are from Knoxville, and many others stop by the many Knoxville hotspots."

"**The bars and clubs in Knoxville are great**. There's a crowd at any club you go to any night of the week. The best times are Sundays at Cotton Eyed Joe's, a line-dancing place. It sounds corny, but it's a lot of fun."

The College Prowler Take On...
Nightlife

UT is extremely lucky to have the Strip, which provides a multitude of places for new people to meet in a convenient location. If you get bored with what the Strip has to offer, the Old City is always an option. There are so many nightspots in Knoxville, there is a pretty good chance you will find something that fits your personality. Most freshmen, however, will not have access to these places until they turn 21. Five years ago, bars on the Strip let just about anybody in. Security has been extremely tightened in recent years due to a few mishaps, and the police keep a close eye on any large concentration of party-goers.

Until your 21st, there are still plenty of places you can go and socialize. Have a good time, and be careful so you can return next year to party!

A-

The College Prowler® Grade on

Nightlife: A-

A high grade in Nightlife indicates that there are many bars and clubs in the area that are easily accessible and affordable. Other determining factors include the number of options for the under-21 crowd and the prevalence of house parties.

Students Speak Out On...
Greek Life

"Being Greek is obviously a choice, but many choices remain after that. There is a fraternity or sorority for everyone at UT. Your freshman year is the best time to explore the option of becoming Greek."

"**We have a large Greek life**, and though they don't totally control the social scene, they do make up a large segment of it. The fraternities are open to anybody, and all girls make their way to the houses, whether or not you're a sorority girl, and most are safe to go to. It's easy to see who the Greeks are, though."

"Greek life is definitely the place to be if you want to get into activities right away. The first pledge semester in almost every Greek organization is the busiest. This really helped me to know what things were like right away. Let's put it this way, **being Greek will not hurt your social life at all**."

"**I am Greek, and I love it**. I would tell anyone coming to UT to at least go through rush—it has made my time at UT a lot better."

"Before you commit to a fraternity, **find out the exacts about dues** so you do not waste time and effort."

"For me, I made a lot of friends in the dorm my freshman year. After that, they all went their separate ways and went to different places, and I never heard from or saw much of them again. It seems this is less likely to happen if you are Greek because **they tend to stick together more**."

"Being Greek is pretty big on campus, but that doesn't mean it segregates people. I'm Greek, but a lot of my best friends are not. It just depends on how open-minded you are about people and things—**you can control how much it dominates your life**."

"If you do not go Greek, it does not mean that you will have an unhappy time at UT. **The school is so big that everyone has plenty of opportunities** if they are willing to work, regardless if they are Greek or not.'"

"**Greek life encompasses 10 percent of the campus**. To those 10 percent that live and breathe it, they are a fairly tight-knit group that generally stays within its own ranks. Greek life throws most of the parties and does a majority of the philanthropic work around campus. They attempt to dominate, but this campus does not care."

"**Being Greek will open many doors** that would be much more difficult to open if you are not Greek. You will have access to a lot of things, not just a social life, that will benefit you as a person."

"**The Greek system at the University of Tennessee is one of the best in the country** and has won many national awards. If going Greek is something that interests you, then definitely consider registering for rush."

"The best part about going Greek is all the people you will meet. They won't be people you forget after graduation; **they will be friends for a lifetime**."

The College Prowler Take On... Greek Life

If going Greek is something that interests you, going through rush is definitely something to consider. At the very least, you will meet people that you will see again and again throughout your college career. Through a Greek organization, you will be able to participate in philanthropies, parties, formals, and the many Greek events that happen throughout the year. If you choose not to do so, you will still have many opportunities at UT to keep you busy, and you will still be able to make many friends.

On paper, it may seem that the number of Greeks are relatively small, and they may not have that much impact on campus. As many students stated, most Greeks are very active and willing to participate in campus events. They, by no means, control everything, but the small percentage of Greeks at UT are very prominent and involved in many successful endeavors. Learn as much as you can about the individual chapters and Greek life in general. Talk with those who have chosen the Greek life, and ask plenty of questions. There is a lot you can do before going through rush to determine if it is for you.

A-

The College Prowler® Grade on

Greek Life: A-

A high grade in Greek Life indicates that sororities and fraternities are not only present, but also active on campus. Other determining factors include the variety of houses available and the respect the Greek community receives from the rest of the campus.

Drug Scene

The Lowdown On...
Drug Scene

Most Prevalent Drugs on Campus:
Alcohol, Marijuana

Drug-Related Referrals:
115

Liquor-Related Referrals:
415

Drug Counseling Programs

Alcoholics Anonymous
(865) 522-9667 or (800) 841-2319

Alanon/Alateen
(865) 525-9040

Centerpointe (residential and outpatient, state-supported)
(865) 523-4704

Dri-Dock Detoxification Unite (state-supported)
(865) 558-5705

Lighthouse Alcohol and Drug Treatment Center (residential, private)
(865) 558-8880

Narcotics Anonymous
(865) 521-1989 or (800) 249-0012

Students Speak Out On...
Drug Scene

"You'll find drugs if you want them, but it's not so bad if you want to avoid the drug scene. It's certainly not a problem that makes the city scary or anything."

"At UT, like any college campus, **there is some drug use**. People will not try to shove it in your face and will not put a lot of pressure on you to do it. People who do drugs are somewhat discreet about it—they slip away, do their thing, and come back. If it isn't something you want to do, you aren't the only one, and they won't force the issue."

"The drug scene on campus has leveled off in recent years since I came here. I remember seeing it all over the place. But **since that time, the drugs have decreased in use**. The people who use drugs, however, use them more extensively now while numbers have dropped."

"Weed is the main drug in the area. Crystal meth is on the rise, but the cops are really cracking down on it. The part of town you're in determines the type of drugs you run into. **X is also very big here**. Typical drugs like crack, coke, and heroine are present, but very underground. You really have to go looking for those and run in those crowds to find them."

"Depending on the circle of friends you spend your time with, **drugs can either be very prominent or non-existent**. It seems like there is not an overwhelming pressure to do drugs, but if you are someone that is against it, you would do best to keep those who do at a distance."

"**You can get whatever you want if you know the right people**. A guy that lived down the hall from me last year had stashes of everything you could imagine. As long as you know someone, you can get anything."

"**I have been able to avoid drugs**, and it's not hard to at all, though you will know someone who does them."

"Those who do drugs usually keep it under wraps. They usually only talk about it to their friends who also do drugs. It isn't extremely visible, but **at some point you may smell marijuana at a party** and spot people who have been smoking it."

"If you want them, **you do not have to search a whole lot to find them** if you know a lot of people. Marijuana is by far the most prominent drug, but for many, it is just a stepping stone to harder drugs."

"When I came to UT, I was näive about drugs and drug use. Now that I have been here several years, I have learned more about it and seen how the whole drug culture operates. **There will be a noticeable difference in those who start using drugs in college** and an academic downturn is just one of many changes."

The College Prowler Take On...
Drug Scene

Most students agree that there is not a lot of pressure to do drugs at UT. For someone who wants drugs, however, they are not impossible to find. You will probably know people that do it, but they probably will never pressure you to do it. Most students agree that the people who choose to do drugs keep it to themselves and their close friends.

Marijuana is the number one cash crop in the state of Tennessee and is easily the cheapest and most readily available drug. A lot of drug users limit their use to marijuana alone and do not use any harder drugs. The harder drugs can be found throughout Knoxville, but are well hidden. You will probably not have many encounters with drugs other than marijuana. With drugs in general, it is easy to maintain your stance once it is made, and people will handle your decisions as an adult the majority of the time.

B-

The College Prowler® Grade on

Drug Scene: B-

A high grade in the Drug Scene indicates that drugs are not a noticeable part of campus life; drug use is not visible, and no pressure to use them seems to exist.

Campus Strictness

The Lowdown On... Campus Strictness

What Are You Most Likely to Get Caught Doing on Campus?

- Basic traffic violations throughout campus
- Parking in an unauthorized area

Students Speak Out On...
Campus Strictness

"The campus police are good at enforcing the rules, but they understand it's a college town and are lenient if you're not doing anything too bad."

"**The main thing campus police hate is attitude**. Think about it—they have a tough job, sometimes dealing with thousands of rude college students. They don't go out and spoil fun for the hell of it—it is their job. If, in any event, you do have an encounter with law enforcement, show them proper respect or they can make life hard for you very quickly. Most officers have an uncanny ability to remember names and faces of particularly offensive subjects, so the second time around will be doubly harsh."

"Campus police don't get involved unless you make a complete fool of yourself in public. As long as you are smart about what you do, you will not get in trouble at all. **You will have to watch out for your RA**—they can be jerks, but most of them are pretty cool about partying, and will even help you get stuff on some rare occasions. Being smart about it will save your butt."

"**The UTPD is not stupid**. They know exactly what goes on in college dorms, on the Strip, or anywhere else on campus. You won't be the first to try and pull a fast one. Most of those who get caught do so because they were stupid, loud, and obvious about it. They won't do daily dorm inspections for alcohol, but if you give them a reason to come in, and they can smell the gin on the carpet, they won't let it go very easily."

"The problem with freshmen and alcohol is that the majority do not know their limits. They guzzle down beer to impress their friends, and it comes back later to bite them in the butt. The RAs have been at UT a while and have an eagle eye for drunk freshmen. **The RAs are responsible for doing something about it and usually do**."

"The cops have came up with some clever law enforcement tactics in the last few years. **They will strategically set up speed traps along some of the longer roads on campus** and will have cops inside popular late-night eateries."

"**UT is dry campus, so there is no liquor allowed in the dorms or on any UT property**, regardless of your age. They are constantly arresting students on the Strip for being publicly intoxicated."

"The campus police are very strict about their drug policies. **They will arrest and kick out people who are caught with drugs**. However, the campus police rarely find anyone who is dumb enough to do drugs in front of them. The drinking enforcement is a joke, except for inside the dorms. RAs will search and hunt day and night to find anyone with alcohol in the dorms. The campus police concentrate their efforts on the fraternities to snuff out all of their drinking."

"**Police are pretty strict if they actually know about what you're doing**. Most of the time, it is hard for them to track all the students we have on campus. There are lots of people, but that only means more people to make friends with. The best idea is not to take anything into a dorm room. If you are caught, it's hell."

"Police are pretty strict, but **if you are smart and sneaky about things, you can get away with a lot**. At parties, as long as things are in a cup, and there isn't anything like a can sitting out, they can't do a thing."

The College Prowler Take On...
Campus Strictness

There was a time when the UT Police were rather lax, but times have changed. Receiving the title "biggest party school" has been a blessing, as well as a curse, in that strictness has definitely increased. There are more police on campus, and they are more than willing to seek out those who are causing trouble. There is a certain level of liability connected with a campus of UT's size, and they are heavily pressured by administration to make UT a safer campus.

Most students will say that with a school of UT's size, it is impossible to totally regulate drinking. The campus police know that if they sought out and punished every crime that was committed, their lives would be those of endless headaches, paperwork, and sleepless nights. As long as UT does not enlist the help of Batman, Spiderman, and Superman to fight campus crime, parties and drinking will inevitably ensue. As long as you are smart about having a good time by knowing your limits, obeying and respecting the law, and staying quiet (a lot of big busts begin as noise violations) you will never come face-to-face with Johnny Law. Be aware of campus rules and policies about alcohol. They are rather strict, and knowledge of the rules might keep you out of trouble.

B

The College Prowler® Grade on

Campus Strictness: B

A high Campus Strictness grade implies an overall lenient atmosphere; police and RAs are fairly tolerant, and the administration's rules are flexible.

Parking

The Lowdown On... Parking

Approximate Parking Permit Cost:

Non-commuter – $241

Commuter – $155

UT Parking Services:

2121 Stephenson Dr.

(865) 974-6031

web.utk.edu/~pso

Student Parking Lot?

Yes

Freshmen Allowed to Park?

Yes

Parking Permits

Commuter

Fraternity (only available to active brothers)

Motorcycle

Non-commuter

Perimeter

Staff

Students who do not register for these permits should register for an "E" tag, which is free, but does not legally allow parking anywhere. It will only reduce the fine because your vehicle is registered with UT.

Common Parking Tickets

Expired Meter – $14 for registered vehicles, $28 for non-registered vehicles.

Fire Lane – $42 tow-away fee, plus $42 citation, and a $3 per day storage fee.

Handicapped Zone – $42 tow-away fee, plus $100 citation, and a $3 per day storage fee.

No Parking Zone – $42 tow-away fee, plus $42 citation, and a $3 per day storage fee.

Did You Know?

Best Places to Find a Parking Spot

Spots in dorm parking lots are relatively easy to find in the late afternoon and on weekends. On weekdays at 9 a.m., they begin to fill up. On game day, you might as well be panning for gold in the Tennessee River. Parking spots will be nearly impossible to find.

Good Luck Getting a Parking Spot Here!

Volunteer Boulevard beside Circle Park and the Humanities building

Students Speak Out On... Parking

"Parking will be a nightmare for you if you are one of those people who must park right in front of your building. If you are okay with walking a short distance to get to and from your car when you park, it is no problem."

"**Parking is the only slightly negative thing about UT**. I'll give it to you straight—they sell more non-commuter tags than there are spaces. Just the same, I was never stranded without a space to park. There will always be a garage, even if it's a mile away. If you're way out there, you can take Blinky (University van service) back to your dorm. They also give out parking tickets like candy if you don't park where you're supposed to park. It's very clear where to park and where not to, so just follow the rules and you won't get 12 tickets like my roommate and I did! Don't worry too much—each ticket is $12, and you can sometimes argue your way out of one."

"The parking scene is one of UT's main problems, but they are working on it. We do have **four parking garages and a bunch of outdoor lots**. As long as you buy a parking permit early, you can generally find a spot."

"**Parking is annoying**. Very few campuses can solve the problem of parking, but if you don't have a car, it's not a big deal. Even if you do, there are ways to get around buying a permit and secret ways to find hidden parking spots."

"**The parking scene on campus is something out of a war picture**. In recent years, the number of parking passes per parking spot has dropped to a more convenient number, but parking during peak hours is still a nightmare, even with two new parking garages built."

"People say it's hard to park, but **it's not nearly as bad as it was when I was a freshman**. I commuted and never had trouble finding a spot. My friends in the dorms were usually all right, too. Just don't be the last one back to campus and don't be afraid to walk."

"A lot of freshmen find a good parking space and avoid driving to keep it. **Always keep your car in check**. A lot of people leave their cars in garages and find them dented, scratched, or vandalized."

"**Parking is a nightmare**—it's definitely the worst part of UT. There are not enough spaces by a long shot. I assume you will be living on campus, which is not as bad as being a commuter. On-campus students choose to walk to as many places as they can, even if they have cars. If you move your car, you are likely never to find another spot. If you don't live on campus, you have to get to campus no less than 30 minutes before your class starts just to find parking, and you will no doubt have to walk three days to get from your car to your class. It's like this on a lot of campuses, though, so don't get too freaked. You learn to live with it."

"I'm not going to lie—parking absolutely sucks. What can you do when you go to a school as large as UT? **It's not really a big deal unless you are a commuter**, and as a freshman, you will have to live on campus where you really don't need a car. By your sophomore year, you'll get used to the campus to learn to work the system. I didn't have my car first semester, and it wasn't a problem at all."

"If you are a freshman considering bringing a car to campus, you may want to reconsider. It is nice not dealing with the hassle and not having to keep up with your car. There won't be much you will have to leave for anyway, since most everything you need is on campus. **Chances are you can bum rides for everywhere else**."

The College Prowler Take On...
Parking

It is rather expensive to obtain a parking pass at UT, and students describe the parking situation as inadequate and rarely reliable. Both the UTPD and City of Knoxville will issue parking tickets, and they can get pretty expensive with habitual parking violations. There are not many college campuses that offer a perfect parking environment, so it is one inconvenience you will have to bear anywhere.

Parking is a classic gripe here at UT. There are even bumper stickers that voice the many parking woes of UT. It is all a game finding the good spots at the good times and avoiding tickets. Of course, if you do not come to UT with a vehicle, it is not your problem. If so, pay attention to which lots you are entitled to and those you are not, and plan ahead for walking distances and spot hunting. Remember, parking a large blue Hummer beside Ayres Hall is the fastest and easiest way to make a generous donation to Parking Services.

D+

The College Prowler® Grade on

Parking: D+

A high grade in this section indicates that parking is both available and affordable, and that parking enforcement isn't overly severe.

Transportation

The Lowdown On... Transportation

Ways to Get Around Town:

Public Transportation

Knoxville Area Transit (KAT)
(865) 637-3000

Sassafras Transportation
(865) 971-4075

Taxi Cabs

Big Orange Express,
(865) 523-3400

Service Special Delivery Co., Inc.
(865) 522-5151

(Taxi Cabs, continued)

College Cab Co.
(865) 523-2537

Car Rentals

Alamo (865) 342-3212
www.alamo.com

Avis (865) 560-5188
www.avis.com

Budget (865) 694-3401
www.budget.com

Edward Jones & Company
(865) 531-6584

Enterprise (865) 212-5609
www.enterprise.com

→

(Car Rentals, continued)

Hertz (865) 970-3010
www.hertz.com

Landoak Rental & Leasing
(865) 966-0801

National (865) 970-2993
www.nationalcar.com

Ted Russell Ford Rent-A-Car
(865) 693-7620

Thrifty (865) 525-1056
www.thrifty.com

U-Save Auto Rental
(865) 693-7620

Wright Curtis OFC
(865) 693-0610

Best Ways to Get Around Town

Friends with cars

KAT

Ways to Get Out of Town:

Airport

McGhee Tyson Airport
PO Box 15600, Knoxville

(865) 342-3000

Airlines Serving Knoxville

American Airlines
(800) 433-7300
www.aa.com

Comair
(800) 354-9822
www.fly-comair.com

Continental Express
(800) 525-0280
www.continental.com

(Airlines Serving Knoxville, continued)

Delta Airlines (800) 221-1212
www.delta.com

Northwest Airlines
(800) 225-2525
www.nwa.com

United Express (800) 241-6522
www.ual.com

US Airways Express
(800) 428-4322
www.usairways.com

How to Get to the Airport

The McGhee Tyson Airport is just south of Knoxville on Route 129.

www.tys.org

Greyhound

Greyhound Bus Lines

100 E Magnolia Ave.
Knoxville, TN 37917

local: (865) 524-0369

national: (800) 231-2222

www.greyhound.com

Amtrak

There is no Amtrak station serving Knoxville. The closest one is in Toccoa, GA.

Toccoa Amtrak Station

47 N Alexandria St.
Toccoa, GA 30577

local: (706) 886-8451

national: (800) USA-RAIL

www.amtrak.com

Students Speak Out On...
Transportation

"A free and very cute trolley runs from the center of campus to downtown, stopping around campus and at the Fort, where most off-campus kids live."

"**Public transportation was not as convenient** until recently when they installed a new bus system around campus. It runs a little beyond schedule, but it beats having to walk over two miles to class."

"**Knoxville Area Transit (KAT) runs many buses** and free trolleys around the city, so getting around town should never be a problem for you."

"**The public bus and free downtown trolley travel through campus constantly**, and many students take advantage of it. We do not have a subway or L train of any kind."

"We have trolleys that run through campus, the Strip, and the Old City every single day, and they're totally free. We also have the KAT buses, which are free for UT freshmen. **The buses run all over Knoxville**. We have a Greyhound bus station and taxis that you can call. The airport, McGhee Tyson Airport, is about 15 minutes from campus, but it's fairly small."

"**The T, which is UT's new transportation system**, is very reliable and easy to use. All of the pick-up spots are clearly marked."

"**The school gives you a free bus pass for the city** of Knoxville that takes you to the mall and stuff."

"**Plenty of people use public transportation**. If you live on campus or near campus, you won't even need it. The strip on Cumberland Avenue has plenty to do and, if worst comes to worst, there are always friends to give you a ride."

"**Most UT students never use public transit** around Knoxville. If there is something you need that is farther than the Strip and you do not have a car, you go with someone who does."

"Your dependence on public transportation depends on your major. If you're studying agriculture where classes are far away, **public transportation is a life saver**. For anything else, it's easier just to walk up 'the hill' to class."

The College Prowler Take On...
Transportation

Although most everything you need will be located within walking distance, the occasional need or want to go further out can be satisfied with multiple transportation options. A car, in most cases, is the best means of getting from point A to point B.

The walks to and from class are not that harsh, and may actually help ward off the "Freshman 15," but "the T" is excellent if you would rather not walk. It is as easy as stepping on and sitting—you do not need a card to board. The only situation that creates an absolute necessity for most students is the ability to travel home for breaks.

A-

The College Prowler® Grade on

Transportation: A-

A high grade for Transportation indicates that campus buses, public buses, cabs, and rental cars are readily-available and affordable. Other determining factors include proximity to an airport and the necessity of transportation.

Weather

The Lowdown On... Weather

Average Temperature:

Fall:	59 °F
Winter:	38 °F
Spring:	57 °F
Summer:	75 °F

Average Precipitation:

Fall:	3.2 in.
Winter:	4.3 in.
Spring:	4.3 in.
Summer:	3.9 in.

Students Speak Out On... Weather

"The weather varies; we have all four seasons. It snows in winter, and it can get really cold, but spring is amazing. Fall is nice, and summer is especially hot, but it's also great."

"People in Knoxville freak out when the weatherman calls for snow. When it begins to fall, they leave work early and hit the grocery stores. As soon as snow hits, the roads will be packed with cars leaving work. Be forewarned—**people in Knoxville cannot drive in snow**. Cars are like elephants on roller-skates."

"**The weather is a weird thing here**. There are times when it is sunny and warm, and the next day it will be freezing. We do have nice fall and springtime weather. It's just the in-between stuff that is different. It is humid here at times, but it's not too bad."

"Canceling class due to snow is extremely rare, but does happen. Even if the local schools have cancelled, UT will try its best to hold classes. **UT campus is one of the first places the Department of Transportation plows**."

"**Weather here is generally hot or bitter cold**. The skies are always a great gray color that never lifts until spring. That is nearly five months of straight gray that drives everyone nuts. You bring clothing for hot summer nights, and then it gradually gets colder from the first month. In winter, around March, it begins to warm up."

"The weather has been horrible this year. **It will be 80 degrees one day and 30 degrees the next**. It's not always like that, though. Generally, the summers are in the high 70s and mid-80s. The spring and fall temperatures hang around 60 degrees and winter temperatures don't often go below 30 degrees. We don't normally get a lot of snow, and when we do get any snow, the whole town shuts down. UT never closes, regardless of whether we have three inches or 30 feet of snow. Your teachers may cancel class, though, and they will probably tell you what their weather policies are at the beginning of the semester."

"**The weather is mild**, with spring and summer averages around 70 to 85 degrees. During the winter, it's about 30 or 40 degrees, and we didn't get a single snowstorm last year. We usually see about three or four good snows each winter."

"My biggest complaint about Knoxville weather is the humidity. **After a light rain, the sun comes out and creates an awful haze**."

"**Expect the unexpected**. Dress in layers and always carry an umbrella. In the winter, it will get into the 30s and in the summer the temperature will be in the 90s. There is a distinct possibility that you will walk to class in the snow one day and wear a T-shirt to class the next."

"The weather is rather mild. We don't get much snow, but if it's cold enough in the winter, **we sometimes get some ice storms**. In the summer, temperatures range from the 80s to the 90s; in winter, I'd say it runs from the 30s to the 50s."

"**Knoxville usually receives two or three good snows** a year. The rest, if any, never accumulate. This will usually happen between January or March. Of course, it often never happens at all."

The College Prowler Take On... Weather

Knoxville weather is pretty mild. None of the four seasons come on very strongly, and neither the snow nor the summer heat will be much of a burden. There will be days you walk to class in a heavy coat and return to your dorm in a T-shirt, so you may want to start swapping summer clothes for some warmer ones during fall break. You will need to start spring semester with heavier clothing, such as sweaters and a thick coat, but you will probably be able to switch over to a light jacket just before Spring Break. The last month or so of classes is usually suitable for short sleeves and shorts. You will need a raincoat or sturdy umbrella year-round.

When, and if, it does snow, don't even think about driving somewhere unless you enjoy mass confusion and an occasional demolition derby (Johnny Knoxville would truly earn his name after attempting to drive through Knoxville amidst falling snow). Knoxville roads will be in a frenzy, and wrecks will be ever abundant. Make sure you finish your homework, however, because UT rarely cancels classes. UT students will pour out of the dorms and have massive snowball fights, which are guaranteed to create long-lasting memories. The fall is absolutely gorgeous, and the campus is beautiful when the leaves begin to fall. Many find the fall months to be most satisfying due to the comfortable temperature and nature. Spring comes with great excitement and is always beautiful on days it does not rain.

B-

The College Prowler® Grade on

Weather: B-

A high Weather grade designates that temperatures are mild and rarely reach extremes, that the campus tends to be sunny rather than rainy, and that weather is fairly consistent rather than unpredictable.

UNIVERSITY OF TENNESSEE

Report Card Summary

B-	ACADEMICS	A-	GUYS
B	LOCAL ATMOSPHERE	A	GIRLS
B	SAFETY & SECURITY	A+	ATHLETICS
B	COMPUTERS	A-	NIGHTLIFE
B+	FACILITIES	A-	GREEK LIFE
B	CAMPUS DINING	B-	DRUG SCENE
A	OFF-CAMPUS DINING	B	CAMPUS STRICTNESS
B-	CAMPUS HOUSING	D+	PARKING
B+	OFF-CAMPUS HOUSING	A-	TRANSPORTATION
D	DIVERSITY	B-	WEATHER

Overall Experience

Students Speak Out On...
Overall Experience

"I wish I had come here right away instead of starting out at a community college. If you are looking for a place to have fun and still get some studying done, UT is definitely the place to go."

"**I love UT**! I am a die-hard Vols fan and wouldn't go anywhere else. If you want somewhere fun and friendly, and somewhere with tons of opportunities, you will love UT."

"I love it. I wouldn't be happier anywhere else. I have no complaints at all, and even though I am far away from home, I never get homesick. **The people at UT are so nice**!"

"**I couldn't have picked a better college**, and I'm so glad I turned down a $12,000 scholarship from another place to go here!"

"**I absolutely love UT**, and I grew up less than 15 minutes away from it. If that's not convincing, I don't know what is!"

"I got a little too caught up in the nightlife of Knoxville my freshman year, but then again, I enjoyed every minute of it. **It's quite an experience to go to class and still be drunk from the night before**."

"For the most part, I like UT. **I've learned it is what you make it**, and you really have to just find your own niche. I go part-time now, and I wish I could be on campus all the time because that is the best way to really get involved and learn about the stuff you will like. Some people don't have that luxury, though, so you have to find other ways to get involved. It really is a good place. Campus is really pretty and, for the most part, the people are really nice. The teachers are helpful, and you just have to remember why you are there in the first place. Don't get too wrapped up in having fun and forget about your education. You will regret it—I've seen it happen."

"My experience at UT has been good, but **Tennessee is suffering because they don't have an income tax**, so many programs are being cut at UT, and tuition is on the rise. It'll be interesting to see how the state legislature deals with the funding problem."

"I'm a very picky person, and I had a list of eight schools I was going to apply to, but **after visiting UT, it was the only school I applied to**. I'm not trying to beef up UT because I know how stressful it is to have to decide on a school, but I like it a lot."

"**I thought it would be real different, too different** from what I am used to at home in Long Island, New York, but I actually found it to be very nice. I love the mountains and the beautiful Tennessee scenery. In the South, there are definitely the accents, and everything is a little more slow paced."

"My experience in school has been a mixture of positives and negatives. The positives have been my social life, experience in the classroom, and overall outcome in life. The negatives have been how **the administration treats me as a number rather than a person**."

"Even though many students often complain about the problems UT has, **most students really do love coming to school here**. I can't think of anywhere else I'd rather be."

"**My experience at UT has been wonderful**. I think that every person can make UT what they want to make it. Getting involved seems to be the thing that separates the people who love UT and those who do not. Even if you do not want to go Greek, I would suggest getting involved in some kind of club."

"Because I have lived so close to UT all of my life, it was not initially somewhere I wanted to go. As soon as I started school and saw what UT had to offer, I felt much better about my choice. I have since become involved in campus activities and gained a solid and useful education. **There are many memories of UT and friends that will be with me for the rest of my life**."

The College Prowler Take On... Overall Experience

UT draws students from all over, and it is little wonder why. UT has a personality all its own. The level of pride and tradition here is among the strongest in the country, and the amount of support Knoxville has for UT is amazing, especially with sports. You will love the laid-back Southern style UT has to offer, and you will enjoy spending time with the people you meet here. Ask any UT alumni about their most positive life experiences, and I guarantee you that most of those experiences will have occurred at UT.

It is understandable to see how UT can appear intimidating on paper, especially to those coming from a small town. There are many different activities to become involved in, and they are yours for the taking if you are willing to make the effort and work hard. The key to success at UT, as well as any college, is to learn to manage your time properly. As long as you remember that education is the main reason for coming to UT and prioritize accordingly, you will be very happy during your college days.

The Inside Scoop

The Lowdown On...
The Inside Scoop

Things I Wish I Knew Before Coming to UT

- The high price of textbooks.
- The parking situation.
- The State of Tennessee's budgeting problems.

Tips to Succeed at UT

Do not let the surrounding environment, which is often carefree and fun-loving, distract you from your goal of obtaining a degree. Not to frighten you, but there will be many faces disappearing the following year because they did not take grades seriously. It is important that you put the time into learning class material so you can get good grades. Those who do not make academics a priority either will not return next year or will not be accepted into their major.

(Tips to Succeed at UT, continued)

Take it upon yourself to become acquainted with your graduation requirements, and take your four-year academic plan very seriously. The ultimate goal of a college education is be able get a return on an investment, meaning you will be able to start a successful career and utilize your skills.

Traditions

Colors

UT's school colors, orange and white, were chosen by Charles Moore, president of the athletic association in 1889. According to Moore, he chose the colors after the orange and white daisies he saw growing on the Hill; it is possible that Moore was color blind, however, since no daisies of such colors are known to exist.

Mascots

The Volunteers get their name from one of Tennessee's most popular nicknames, "the Volunteer State." The nickname derives from the overwhelming number of Tennessee citizens volunteering for military service in past wars.

Smokey, a bluetick coonhound, was instated as the official live UT mascot in 1953. The school chose a hound because the breed is native to Tennessee, and according to the UT Web site, the dog's "small stature and loud baying represent a unique combination."

Finding a Job or Internship

The Lowdown On... Finding a Job or Internship

If you're worried that you won't be able to find a job when you leave UT, you're not alone. Fortunately for everyone, there is a wonderful career services center on campus to help you with any questions or concerns that you might have.

Career Services Office

100 Dunford Hall

(865) 974-6947

Advice

Use connections from teachers and friends. Keep a close eye on the Career Services Web site (*career.utk.edu*). Not only do they have some generally helpful information, but they are constantly updating the schedule of workshops and other services that may be the difference between finding the job of your dreams or the job of your nightmares. Also, as long as you register your job status after you graduate, you will be eligible for alumni services from the Career Services Center.

Career Center Resources & Services

Career classes

Career counseling

Job search preparation

On-campus interviewing

Resume assistance

UT alumni profiles

Web job listings

College Republicans
College Student Personnel Association
Criminal Law Society
Cycling Club
Daily Beacon
Dance Marathon
Equestrian Team
Fencing Club
First Priority
Habitat for Humanity
Ice Hockey
Indian-American Association
Institute of Transportation Engineers
Inter-Fraternity Council
International Law Society
International Student Council
Intervarsity Christian Fellowship
Japanese Club
Jewish Student Center
Knoxville Country Dancers
Lacrosse Club, Men's
Latter Day Saints Student Association
Law Women
Learning Communities
Logistics and Transportation Association
Love United Gospel Choir
Lutheran Campus Ministries
Martial Arts Club
Minority Advisors Program
Muslim Student Association
NAACP
National Society of Black Engineers
Navigators
Orthodox Christian Fellowship
Partners in Sports
Phoenix Literary Art Magazine
Plant, Soil, and Environmental Science
Poultry Science Club
Presbyterian Student Center
Progressive Student Alliance
PRSSA
Racquetball Club
Reformed University Fellowship
Students in Free Enterprise
Tenn. Assoc. for Public Interest Law
Ultimate Frisbee Club, Men's
Undergraduate Nutrition Student Association
Water Polo Club

The Best & Worst

The Ten **BEST** Things About UT

1. The rowdy and raucous Neyland Stadium
2. Caring and compassionate professors
3. A wide variety of Greek organizations to choose from
4. Old City
5. The free downtown trolly
6. The friendly and outgoing Knoxville residents
7. The abundance of shool spirit shown by students and locals
8. State-of-the-art facilities (both educational and recreational)
9. Volunteer football
10. Only and hour's drive from the Great SmokyMountains

The Ten **WORST** Things About UT

1. Large class sizes (especially for general courses)
2. The recent crackdown by campus security
3. No parking
4. The unpredictable (and often way too humid) weather
5. Lack of diversity
6. Rising tuition
7. Stuck-up individuals (snotty hotties)
8. Lack of food quality on campus
9. Meal plan does not carry over money
10. Overcrowded library computer labs

Visiting

The Lowdown On... Visiting

Hotel Information:

Budget Inn
5334 Central Ave. Pike
(865) 688-1010
www.comfortinn.com
Distance from Campus: 5.7 miles
Price Range: $55–$65

Crowne Plaza
401 Summit Hill Dr.
(865) 522-2600
www.radisson.com
Distance from Campus: 2.0 miles
Price Range: $99–$106

Hampton Inn-West
9128 Executive Park Blvd.
(865) 693-1101
www.hamptoninn.com
Distance from Campus: 10.7 miles
Price Range: $99–$104

Hilton Knoxville
501 West Church Ave.
(865) 523-2300
www.hiltonworldwide.com
Distance from Campus: 1.2 miles
Price Range: $99–$149

→

Holiday Inn Select-Downtown
525 Henley St.
(865) 522-2800
www.holiday-inn.com
Distance from Campus: 1.5 miles
Price Range: $115–$125

Howard Johnson Plaza
7621 Kingston Pike
(865) 693-8111
www.hojo.com
Distance from Campus: 6.8 miles
Price Range: $60–$68

The Knoxville Marriott
500 Hill Ave. SE
(865) 637-1234
www.marriott.com
Distance from Campus: 1.9 miles
Price Range: $99–$149

Maplehurst Bed & Breakfast
800 West Hill Ave.
(865) 523-7773
www.maplehurstinn.com
Distance from Campus:
1 mile
Price Range: $79–$149

Red Roof Inn-West
209 Advantage Place
(865) 691-1664
www.redroof.com
Distance from Campus: 11.1 miles
Price Range: $54–$64

Super 8 Motel
6200 Papermill Dr.
(865) 584-8511
www.super8.com
Distance from Campus: 6.1 miles
Price Range: $49–$54

Parkside Inn Hotel
208 Market Place Lane
(865) 531-1900
www.wyndham.com
Distance from Campus: 11.3 miles
Price Range: $79–$89

Take a Campus Virtual Tour

http://admissions.utk.edu/virtualtour

To Schedule a Group Information Session or Interview

There are three main ways that you can go about scheduling a campus tour at UT. The first option is to schedule your tour over the Internet at *admissions.utk.edu/undergraduate/tours8.shtml*. If you are computer savvy, but don't feel like going through the trouble of filling out the campus-tour forms, you can also send an e-mail to admisgs@gw.utk.edu, and do things that way. If you have no proficiency whatsoever with the ol' computing box, you can also call to schedule an interview at (865) 974-2184.

Important Tip

When it comes to online assistance, the UT Web site is wonderful, to say the least. Make sure to check out the school's official site thoroughly. Not only do they have a virtual campus tour that includes audio, they also have an online walking tour of campus. It's easy to get familiar with the University before you even step foot there.

Directions to Campus

From the Atlanta/Chattanooga Area

- Follow I-75 North to I-40 East. In Knoxville, take the James White Parkway Exit (#388 A).
- Follow 158 W (Neyland Drive/University of Tennessee) to the third traffic light.
- Turn right onto Lake Loudon Boulevard.
- Follow Lake Loudon to the second traffic light.
- Follow Volunteer Boulevard to the second traffic light and turn right onto Cumberland Avenue.
- At the first traffic light on Cumberland Avenue, turn right onto Phillip Fulmer Way.
- The University Center Parking Garage will be on the right. (Look for the Public Parking sign and the brick wall that has a number of automated teller machines.)

From the Nashville Area

- Follow I-40 East to the James White Parkway Exit (#388 A).
- Follow 158 W (Neyland Drive/University of Tennessee) to the third traffic light.
- Turn right onto Lake Loudon Boulevard.
- Follow Lake Loudon to the second traffic light.
- Turn right onto Volunteer Boulevard.
- Follow Volunteer Boulevard to the second traffic light and turn right onto Cumberland Avenue.
- At the first traffic light on Cumberland Avenue, turn right onto Phillip Fulmer Way.
- The University Center Parking Garage will be on the right. (Look for the Public Parking sign and the brick wall that has a number of automated teller machines.)

From the Lexington/Cincinnati Area

- Follow I-75 South to 275 South (Knoxville).
- Follow 275 South to I-40 East (Asheville).
- Follow I-40 East to the James White Parkway Exit (#388 A).
- Follow 158 W (Neyland Drive/University of Tennessee) to the third traffic light.

(From the Lexington/Cincinnati Area, continued)

- Turn right onto Lake Loudon Boulevard.
- Follow Lake Loudon to the second traffic light.
- Turn right onto Volunteer Boulevard.
- Follow Volunteer Boulevard to the second traffic light and turn right onto Cumberland Avenue.
- At the first traffic light on Cumberland Avenue, turn right onto Phillip Fulmer Way.
- The University Center Parking Garage will be on the right. (Look for the Public Parking sign and the brick wall that has a number of automated teller machines.)

From the North Carolina Area

- Follow I-40 West to the James White Parkway Exit (#388 A).
- Follow 158 W (Neyland Drive/University of Tennessee) to the third traffic light.
- Turn right onto Lake Loudon Boulevard.
- Follow Lake Loudon to the second traffic light.
- Turn right onto Volunteer Boulevard.
- Follow Volunteer Boulevard to the second traffic light and turn right onto Cumberland Avenue.
- At the first traffic light on Cumberland Avenue, turn right onto Phillip Fulmer Way.
- The University Center Parking Garage will be on the right. (Look for the Public Parking sign and the brick wall that has a number of automated teller machines.)

From the Tri-Cities, TN Area

- Follow I-81 South to I-40 West.
- Take the James White Parkway Exit (#388 A).
- Follow 158 W (Neyland Drive/University of Tennessee) to the third traffic light.
- Turn right onto Lake Loudon Boulevard.
- Follow Lake Loudon to the second traffic light.
- Turn right onto Volunteer Boulevard.
- Follow Volunteer Boulevard to the second traffic light and turn right onto Cumberland Avenue.

(From the Tri-Cities, TN Area, continued)

- At the first traffic light on Cumberland Avenue, turn right onto Phillip Fulmer Way.
- The University Center Parking Garage will be on the right. (Look for the Public Parking sign and the brick wall that has a number of automated teller machines.)

Words to Know

Academic Probation – A suspension imposed on a student if he or she fails to keep up with the school's minimum academic requirements. Those unable to improve their grades after receiving this warning can face dismissal.

Beer Pong/Beirut – A drinking game involving cups of beer arranged in a pyramid shape on each side of a table. The goal is to get a ping pong ball into one of the opponent's cups by throwing the ball or hitting it with a paddle. If the ball lands in a cup, the opponent is required to drink the beer.

Bid – An invitation from a fraternity or sorority to 'pledge' (join) that specific house.

Blue-Light Phone – Brightly-colored phone posts with a blue light bulb on top. These phones exist for security purposes and are located at various outside locations around most campuses. In an emergency, a student can pick up one of these phones (free of charge) to connect with campus police or a security escort.

Campus Police – Police who are specifically assigned to a given institution. Campus police are typically not regular city officers; they are employed by the university in a full-time capacity.

Club Sports – A level of sports that falls somewhere between varsity and intramural. If a student is unable to commit to a varsity team but has a lot of passion for athletics, a club sport could be a better, less intense option. Even less demanding, intramural (IM) sports often involve no traveling and considerably less time.

Cocaine – An illegal drug. Also known as "coke" or "blow," cocaine often resembles a white crystalline or powdery substance. It is highly addictive and dangerous.

Common Application – An application with which students can apply to multiple schools.

Course Registration – The period of official class selection for the upcoming quarter or semester. Prior to registration, it is best to prepare several back-up courses in case a particular class becomes full. If a course is full, students can place themselves on the waitlist, although this still does not guarantee entry.

Division Athletics – Athletic classifications range from Division I to Division III. Division IA is the most competitive, while Division III is considered to be the least competitive.

Dorm – A dorm (or dormitory) is an on-campus housing facility. Dorms can provide a range of options from suite-style rooms to more communal options that include shared bathrooms. Most first-year students live in dorms. Some upperclassmen who wish to stay on campus also choose this option.

Early Action – An application option with which a student can apply to a school and receive an early acceptance response without a binding commitment. This system is becoming less and less available.

Early Decision – An application option that students should use only if they are certain they plan to attend the school in question. If a student applies using the early decision option and is admitted, he or she is required and bound to attend that university. Admission rates are usually higher among students who apply through early decision, as the student is clearly indicating that the school is his or her first choice.

Ecstasy – An illegal drug. Also known as "E" or "X," ecstasy looks like a pill and most resembles an aspirin. Considered a party drug, ecstasy is very dangerous and can be deadly.

Ethernet – An extremely fast Internet connection available in most university-owned residence halls. To use an Ethernet connection properly, a student will need a network card and cable for his or her computer.

Fake ID – A counterfeit identification card that contains false information. Most commonly, students get fake IDs with altered birthdates so that they appear to be older than 21 (and therefore of legal drinking age). Even though it is illegal, many college students have fake IDs in hopes of purchasing alcohol or getting into bars.

Frosh – Slang for "freshman" or "freshmen."

Hazing – Initiation rituals administered by some fraternities or sororities as part of the pledging process. Many universities have outlawed hazing due to its degrading, and sometimes dangerous, nature.

Intramurals (IMs) – A popular, and usually free, sport league in which students create teams and compete against one another. These sports vary in competitiveness and can include a range of activities—everything from billiards to water polo. IM sports are a great way to meet people with similar interests.

Keg – Officially called a half-barrel, a keg contains roughly 200 12-ounce servings of beer.

LSD – An illegal drug, also known as acid, this hallucinogenic drug most commonly resembles a tab of paper.

Marijuana – An illegal drug, also known as weed or pot; along with alcohol, marijuana is one of the most commonly-found drugs on campuses across the country.

Major –The focal point of a student's college studies; a specific topic that is studied for a degree. Examples of majors include physics, English, history, computer science, economics, business, and music. Many students decide on a specific major before arriving on campus, while others are simply "undecided" until declaring a major. Those who are extremely interested in two areas can also choose to double major.

Meal Block – The equivalent of one meal. Students on a meal plan usually receive a fixed number of meals per week. Each meal, or "block," can be redeemed at the school's dining facilities in place of cash. Often, a student's weekly allotment of meal blocks will be forfeited if not used.

Minor – An additional focal point in a student's education. Often serving as a complement or addition to a student's main area of focus, a minor has fewer requirements and prerequisites to fulfill than a major. Minors are not required for graduation from most schools; however some students who want to explore many different interests choose to pursue both a major and a minor.

Mushrooms – An illegal drug. Also known as "'shrooms," this drug resembles regular mushrooms but is extremely hallucinogenic.

Off-Campus Housing – Housing from a particular landlord or rental group that is not affiliated with the university. Depending on the college, off-campus housing can range from extremely popular to non-existent. Students who choose to live off campus are typically given more freedom, but they also have to deal with possible subletting scenarios, furniture, bills, and other issues. In addition to these factors, rental prices and distance often affect a student's decision to move off campus.

Office Hours – Time that teachers set aside for students who have questions about coursework. Office hours are a good forum for students to go over any problems and to show interest in the subject material.

Pledging – The early phase of joining a fraternity or sorority, pledging takes place after a student has gone through rush and received a bid. Pledging usually lasts between one and two semesters. Once the pledging period is complete and a particular student has done everything that is required to become a member, that student is considered a brother or sister. If a fraternity or a sorority would decide to "haze" a group of students, this initiation would take place during the pledging period.

Private Institution – A school that does not use tax revenue to subsidize education costs. Private schools typically cost more than public schools and are usually smaller.

Prof – Slang for "professor."

Public Institution – A school that uses tax revenue to subsidize education costs. Public schools are often a good value for in-state residents and tend to be larger than most private colleges.

Quarter System (or Trimester System) – A type of academic calendar system. In this setup, students take classes for three academic periods. The first quarter usually starts in late September or early October and concludes right before Christmas. The second quarter usually starts around early to mid–January and finishes up around March or April. The last academic quarter, or "third quarter," usually starts in late March or early April and finishes up in late May or Mid-June. The fourth quarter is summer. The major difference between the quarter system and semester system is that students take more, less comprehensive courses under the quarter calendar.

RA (Resident Assistant) – A student leader who is assigned to a particular floor in a dormitory in order to help to the other students who live there. An RA's duties include ensuring student safety and providing assistance wherever possible.

Recitation – An extension of a specific course; a review session. Some classes, particularly large lectures, are supplemented with mandatory recitation sessions that provide a relatively personal class setting.

Rolling Admissions – A form of admissions. Most commonly found at public institutions, schools with this type of policy continue to accept students throughout the year until their class sizes are met. For example, some schools begin accepting students as early as December and will continue to do so until April or May.

Room and Board – This figure is typically the combined cost of a university-owned room and a meal plan.

Room Draw/Housing Lottery – A common way to pick on-campus room assignments for the following year. If a student decides to remain in university-owned housing, he or she is assigned a unique number that, along with seniority, is used to determine his or her housing for the next year.

Rush – The period in which students can meet the brothers and sisters of a particular chapter and find out if a given fraternity or sorority is right for them. Rushing a fraternity or a sorority is not a requirement at any school. The goal of rush is to give students who are serious about pledging a feel for what to expect.

Semester System – The most common type of academic calendar system at college campuses. This setup typically includes two semesters in a given school year. The fall semester starts around the end of August or early September and concludes before winter vacation. The spring semester usually starts in mid-January and ends in late April or May.

Student Center/Rec Center/Student Union – A common area on campus that often contains study areas, recreation facilities, and eateries. This building is often a good place to meet up with fellow students; depending on the school, the student center can have a huge role or a non-existent role in campus life.

Student ID – A university-issued photo ID that serves as a student's key to school-related functions. Some schools require students to show these cards in order to get into dorms, libraries, cafeterias, and other facilities. In addition to storing meal plan information, in some cases, a student ID can actually work as a debit card and allow students to purchase things from bookstores or local shops.

Suite – A type of dorm room. Unlike dorms that feature communal bathrooms shared by the entire floor, suites offer bathrooms shared only among the suite. Suite-style dorm rooms can house anywhere from two to ten students.

TA (Teacher's Assistant) – An undergraduate or grad student who helps in some manner with a specific course. In some cases, a TA will teach a class, assist a professor, grade assignments, or conduct office hours.

Undergraduate – A student in the process of studying for his or her bachelor's degree.

ABOUT THE AUTHOR

As a lifetime resident of East Tennessee, and a fifth-year senior at the University of Tennessee, I have spent a lifetime absorbing the culture here. I have been fortunate enough to experience other cities and colleges in small enough doses to make me realize how great I have had it in Knoxville all along. While I have given many a high school senior advice about pursuing further education, College Prowler has allowed me to reach a broader audience to share my experience and knowledge.

I currently plan to graduate with a BA in economics, as well as a business minor. I feel that UT has started to prepare me for my ultimate career aspiration of becoming an entrepreneur. I believe that the lessons I have learned outside of the classroom are equally as valuable as textbooks and professors. Among my greatest memories are the beautiful, autumn game days I spent cheering on the Volunteers, the practical jokes I am still laughing about that I played on my fraternity brothers, and the night I spent throwing homecoming-float pomps at the wonderful girl who would soon after become the love of my life.

I hope that the knowledge I have shared with you will prove advantageous as you embark on your college career. It was with purpose that I included carefully selected excerpts of student insight. Mere statistical information and college brochures alone do not truly reflect the environment you are about to enter, and you have made a wise choice by choosing College Prowler. My goal throughout this book was to answer the questions that take others a semester, or in some cases years as a student, to learn. If you have any further questions or comments, please contact me by e-mail.

Jacob W. Williams
jacobwilliams@collegeprowler.com

California Colleges

California dreamin'?

This book is a must have for you!

California Colleges
7¼" X 10", 762 Pages Paperback
$29.95 Retail
1-59658-501-3

Stanford, UC Berkeley, Caltech—California is home to some of America's greatest institutes of higher learning. *California Colleges* gives the lowdown on 24 of the best, side by side, in one prodigious volume.

New England Colleges

Looking for peace in the Northeast?
Pick up this regional guide to New England!

NEW ENGLAND COLLEGES
7¼" X 10", 1015 Pages Paperback
$29.95 Retail
1-59658-504-8

New England is the birthplace of many prestigious universities, and with so many to choose from, picking the right school can be a tough decision. With inside information on over 34 competive Northeastern schools, *New England Colleges* provides the same high-quality information prospective students expect from College Prowler in one all-inclusive, easy-to-use reference.

Schools of the South

Headin' down south? This book will help you find your way to the perfect school!

SCHOOLS OF THE SOUTH
7¼" X 10", 773 Pages Paperback
$29.95 Retail
1-59658-503-X

Southern pride is always strong. Whether it's across town or across state, many Southern students are devoted to their home sweet home. *Schools of the South* offers an honest student perspective on 36 universities available south of the Mason-Dixon.

Need More Help?

Do you have more questions about this school? Can't find a certain statistic? College Prowler is here to help. We are the best source of college information out there. We have a network of thousands of students who can get the latest information on any school to you ASAP. E-mail us at info@collegeprowler.com with your college-related questions.

E-Mail Us Your College-Related Questions!

Check out ***www.collegeprowler.com*** for more details.
1-800-290-2682

College Prowler®

Pros and Cons

Still can't figure out if this is the right school for you? You've already read through this in-depth guide; why not list the pros and cons? It will really help with narrowing down your decision and determining whether or not this school is right for you.

Pros	**Cons**
....	....
....	....
....	....
....	....
....	....
....	....
....	....
....	....
....	....
....	....
....	....
....	....
....	....

COLLEGE PROWLER®

Pros and Cons

Still can't figure out if this is the right school for you? You've already read through this in-depth guide; why not list the pros and cons? It will really help with narrowing down your decision and determining whether or not this school is right for you.

Pros	Cons
....	....
....	....
....	....
....	....
....	....
....	....
....	....
....	....
....	....
....	....
....	....
....	....
....	....

Notes

Notes

Notes

Notes

COLLEGE PROWLER®

Notes

Notes

Notes

Notes

Notes

Notes

Notes

Notes

Notes

Notes

Notes

Notes

Notes

Notes

Notes

Notes

Notes

Notes

Notes

Notes

Notes

COLLEGE PROWLER®

Notes

COLLEGE PROWLER®